MIRACLE TOWN

*Creating America's Bavarian Village
in Leavenworth, Washington*

Recollections of Ted Price
As Told to John Miller

~

Published by
Price & Rodgers
Vancouver, Washington

ISBN 0-9651206-0-0 Paperback
ISBN 0-9651206-1-9 Hardcover
Publisher's Cataloging in Publication *(prepared by Quality Books, Inc.)*
Price, Ted
    Miracle Town: creating America's Bavarian village in Leavenworth, Washington/recollections of Ted Price, as told to John Miller.
        p. cm.
        1. Tourist trade and city planning—Washington (State)—Leavenworth. 2. Community development—Washington (State)—Leavenworth. 3. Leavenworth (Wash.)—History. I. Miller, John (John G.) II. Title.

    G.155.W37P75 1996   979.7'59 QBI96-20121

Library of Congress Catalog Card Number 96-092027

General Editor: Carolyn M. Buan, Writing & Editing Services, Portland, Oregon
Book Design: Jeanne E. Galick, Graphic Design, Portland, Oregon
This book is set in Adobe Garamond and Bembo

Front cover photograph by Gary Schimelfenig (At Mai Fest: Tirolean Dancers, Portland, Oregon)
Back cover photographs by Walt Rembold; bottom photo by Richard Barrington
Inside front cover/overleaf photograph by Craig Ingle

Printed and Bound in Hong Kong by C & C Offset Printing Co., Ltd. Hong Kong • Tokyo • New York • Portland

To my best friend and partner, Robert F. Rodgers;
my beloved mother, Hope Beatrice Miller Price;
my father, Kent Adams Price and
A. Carolyn Gertrude Schutte

~

~

Acknowledgments

I want to express my deepest gratitude to the people of Leavenworth, past and present, whose heart and spirit transformed their dying town into a Bavarian village, and who continue to bring inspiration and enjoyment to millions of visitors. It is impossible to list the contribution of everyone who helped me prepare this book, but the following deserve special mention.

• Robert F. Rodgers, for his creative ideas, guidance, support, unbounded patience and not least, his humor throughout.

• John Miller, a friend who worked every step of the way with me in writing this book for more than two and one-half years. During much of that time we met daily or weekly, conducted interviews and made many trips to Leavenworth. John not only gave unselfishly of his time, talent and knowledge of publishing—he brought to our task a sensitivity and set of deep spiritual principles that informs every page.

• Richard Barrington, for his years of unstinting dedication in producing our video documentaries on Leavenworth—for script writing, filming, editing and narration—and for his generous contribution of photographs for this book, many of which were taken from his professional collection and some of which were produced on special assignment.

• Walt Rembold who, often with his daughter Donna, worked with me from 1960 to the early 1980s to create a fine collection of photographs documenting the Bavarian vision as it became a reality.

• Thomas L. Greene, Jr., who provided his historical collection of photographs taken over fifty years ago.

• Jim Anctil, another friend, who organized thousands of items of archival and research materials, wrote a partial account of the Leavenworth story and helped transcribe video interviews of townspeople.

I salute all the people of Leavenworth who freely and enthusiastically cooperated in being interviewed these past several years. Their stories, recorded in video or audio form, attest to a fervent community spirit that is at the heart of the miracle of Leavenworth. Their interviews will be preserved for future generations in the Price & Rodgers Historical Leavenworth Collection. I have quoted from many of them in the book.

The following people gave generously of themselves—being interviewed, making suggestions or contributing in some way to this project:

Aron Abrahamson
Ren & Adriene Adam
Helga Barrington
The Boyd Family
Arleen Blackburn
Bob Brender
Mike Brickert
Harriet Bullitt
Harry & Marge Butcher
Mike Cecka
Daphne Clark-Harper
Phil Clayton
Betty Crosta
Eleanor Culling
Wilfred Davy
Karen & Virgina Dean
Jack Dorsey
Tim Easterly
John Espelund
Louis Flannery

Rev. Carl Florea
Jeff & Liz Gauger
Chris Gibbs
Rick Harmon
Joy Henson
Mary Lou Hunt
Joan James
Laura Jobin
Bob & Nola Johnson
Jay & Connie Johnson
Rob & Nancy Johnson
Dr. John & Anne Koenig
Russell & Vera Lee
Jack & Eulalia Luckett
Archie & Ester Marlin
Ken Marson
Dr. Ann Martin
Will Martinell
Don May
Janet Motteler
Diane Norman

Fanny Pashkowski
LaVerne Peterson
Frances Reed
The Rembold Family
Ed & Pat Rutledge
Liz Saunders
June Schoenhofen
Scotty Scott
Rod & Anne Simpson
James Strassmaier
Dick & Rena Stroup
Dr. Bill Thetford
Jane Turnbull
Heinz Ulbricht
Delores Van Valkenburgh
Owen & Pauline Watson
Emery Wechselberger
Bill & Diane Wells
Wilfred R. Woods
Mel Wyles

I am also indebted to the professional and amateur photographers whose work greatly enriches these pages. In addition to the photographs from my private collection, those of the following men and women were used:

Richard Barrington
Jim Corwin
Eleanor Culling
Don Eastman
Cliff Ellis

Jeanne E. Galick
Thomas L. Greene, Jr.
Craig Ingle
Bob Miller
Steve Nickols

Walt & Donna Rembold
Michael W. Siegrist, Sr.
Gary Schimelfenig
Dr. Bob Smith

Finally, I wish to thank *The Leavenworth Echo, The Seattle Times, Smith-Western Postcard Company* and *The Wenatchee Daily World*. Complete photography credits appear on page 187.

Inevitably, in a work of this nature errors and omissions will occur. Besides factual mistakes, I am concerned about the spelling of names. For future revisions of this book I invite readers' comments, including corrections of factual errors. When writing me, include your name, address and phone number. To assist in distinguishing between historical fact and hearsay, please give your reference for the corrections. Send these to: Price & Rodgers, c/o John Miller, Box 2821, Portland, Oregon 97208.

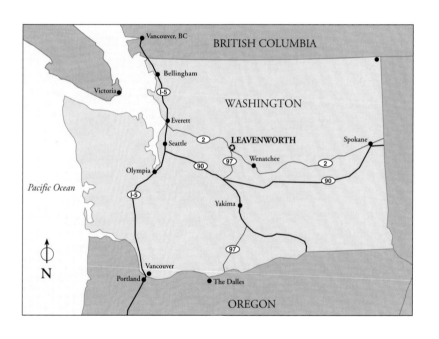

~

Contents

Front Street in the 1950s

Front Street in the 1990s

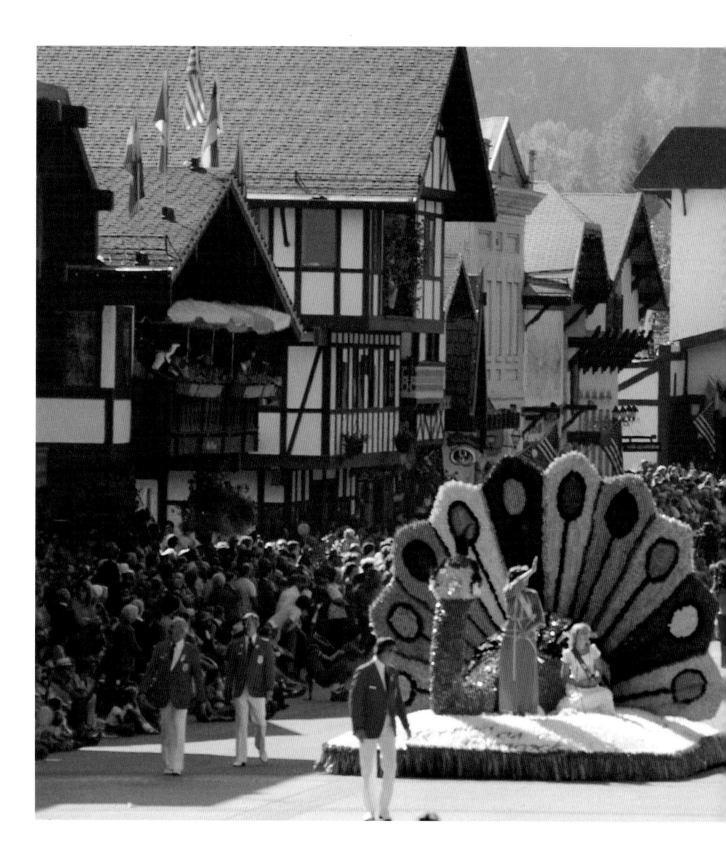

Introduction

By John Miller

The mountains and valleys of the Leavenworth area bear a striking resemblance to the Bavarian and Swiss Alps, but it was not until Ted Price and Bob Rodgers arrived in 1960 that a Bavarian theme was adopted in the area's architecture and cultural activities. The two men initiated the theme first at their restaurant and motel at Cole's Corner 15 miles from Leavenworth and later in the town itself.

Ted and Bob enjoy a rare kind of partnership: it is impossible to tell where the contributions of one leave off and those of the other begin. In a typical understatement Bob once said, "I did have a part in various aspects of Leavenworth's transformation, but for the most part it was Ted's doing. You might say I was his support—I did what I could."

In writing this book, Ted refers to Bavarian Leavenworth as "a miracle of giving," but the miracle he refers to is not the physical transformation of a dying town into a charming Bavarian village. Rather, it is the spirit that lies behind the transformation—the creative powers, imagination, intuition and inner vision that motivated and guided the people of a small, depressed town committed to self-improvement.

Like all of us, Ted Price has lived a life filled with apparent contradictions. Ted is a dreamer, a successful businessman and a deeply spiritual person. He has found guidance in the life and teachings of Jesus, as well as in the more modern spiritual lights of Charles and Myrtle Fillmore, founders of Unity, and of Joel Goldsmith, whose message The Infinite Way has inspired my own life. In particular, Goldsmith taught that all life, all power, all supply flow from an invisible motivating energy he called "consciousness," and he said, "The grace of God has sent men and women to earth in all ages to show the world the miracle of grace."

In Leavenworth, Ted believes, he saw this energy or force in action as he repeatedly witnessed a kind of serendipitous coming together of the right people, skills, talents and sources of financial support at critical junctures in the town's transformation to a Bavarian village. The initial remodeling, he tells us, was accomplished without any government money whatsoever. When money was needed it just seemed to appear. The same phenomenon occurred when the need was for professional knowledge or skills. The right people with the talents and abilities most needed seemed to appear in town at just the right moment.

Perhaps it is his trust in this unseen power that enabled Ted to hold so tenaciously to the notion that Leavenworth *could* succeed as a tourist destination. As his story reveals, he not only planted the idea of a Bavarian theme town in the minds of the townspeople—he wouldn't rest until it was realized in every minute detail. Russell Lee, former owner/editor of *The Leavenworth Echo*, once said, "I always maintained that if it wasn't for Ted's dream, and [his partner] Bob right along with him, it's questionable whether any of this would have ever happened...."

Once Ted told a group, "Castles on the ground, it is said, are not built until we first dream about them. Every structure is first the dream of the architect. Dreams that are realized become an inspiration to others for new endeavors....Let's not allow seeds of doubt to destroy our dreams and aspirations."

Ted was "the dreamer" who initiated so much that has become a reality in Leavenworth, and he was involved in almost every major project from the beginning. In fact, Ted and his partner Bob Rodgers invested so completely in the vision of a Bavarian Leavenworth that for years they were often on the verge of bankruptcy. As events seemed to steamroller along and Leavenworth was transformed, Ted did not seek personal recognition. While he was skilled at generating widescale publicity for Leavenworth, he tried to avoid it for himself. Sometimes he and Bob led and served openly, but often they preferred to remain behind the scenes and, like two Johnny Appleseeds, plant ideas for change in the minds and imaginations of others.

Artists, prophets and visionaries are celebrated, yes, but rarely are they understood when they first appear in a community. No one with a creative mind is ever received openly and gladly by the world at large, because original ideas mean that people's attitudes must change and their lives will never be the same as before. A radical change means we have to be willing to let go, to risk losing some control over our lives, to embrace the unknown in life. Our defense against such a threatening change sometimes is to attack the messenger who comes with new ideas.

Thus, along with their success, Ted and Bob encountered misunderstanding, obstacles and difficulties, resentment and jealousy. Bob has said, "I think one of the biggest disappointments for Ted was the distrust that people had of him. It's probably cost him thousands of nights of missed sleep."

Now that the dream is a reality, it is fitting that Ted should tell his story. And it is typical of him that in doing so he has looked beyond any past discouragements and adversity to write a tribute to the people of Leavenworth.

To Ted, the miracle of giving for each of us is an attitude toward ourself and others. It is a way of living that arises out of openness, selflessness and cooperation, that encourages each person to express his or her greatest abilities and talents. More than anything else it is the true understanding that what we give to another, we give to ourselves.

Although Ted and Bob are no longer active in the affairs of Leavenworth, they are present in spirit, and there they will always be.

~

*"Miracles occur naturally as expressions of love...
they are everyone's right.
A miracle is never lost.
It may touch many people you have not even met
and produce undreamed of changes in situations
of which you are not even aware."*

— A Course In Miracles

Impossible Dreams
and Foolish Ideas

"...the town had almost gotten to be a ghost town, so many of the buildings downtown were boarded up....Leavenworth was a dead town economically."

—*Walt Rembold*

"What you see here today is the result of a group of very dedicated people with a vision for the future."

—*Bob Brender*

Have you ever had an impossible dream? Wished for a miracle? Been told that you had foolish ideas? In Leavenworth, Washington, we had many impossible dreams and foolish ideas. And we believed in miracles.

This is a story about a vision that came true—about the transformation of Leavenworth from a town that was dying into a Bavarian village. I believe the story proves that ordinary people like you and me are wonderfully capable of bringing magic, beauty and enjoyment into the lives of others.

Every first-time visitor to Leavenworth wonders, "How did this happen? How in the world did such a small town *do* all of this?" The story of the Leavenworth miracle has never been told fully, and indeed perhaps it never will be, for it is many stories involving most of the town's residents and dozens of people from other places.

When I first considered writing the Leavenworth story, I thought that a full and balanced account could best be told jointly with longtime Leavenworth resident Pauline Watson. We sometimes held opposing views, but we were united in many important ways. Unfortunately, such a collaborative work was not possible.

Our impossible dream— transforming a near ghost town into a thriving Bavarian village. (Above) Front Street in 1964. (Below) Front Street today. Over a million people visit Leavenworth each year.

I do not claim that my account is a definitive history. Rather, it is *my* story: my recollection of what happened and of the roles my partner Bob Rodgers and I played in Leavenworth's transformation, first when we introduced the idea of a Bavarian theme town and helped develop it, then as we urged people to accept tourism as the way to prevent economic disaster from destroying the town.

Any telling of this story must include the people who dared to dream of what their town might be and who then risked everything to fulfill their dreams. These are the people who overcame difficult and sometimes hopeless personal obstacles to join with others in creating an authentic Bavarian village in central Washington.

More than anything else, the secret of Leavenworth lies in giving. People gave and gave and gave—of their time, their creative talents, their professional abilities, their labor, their hearts and goodwill. More tellingly,

they gave hard-earned, even borrowed, money—often at quite a sacrifice to themselves and their families. Of course there were also critics and detractors, whose main contribution was, unwittingly, to renew the faith and resolve of those who believed the impossible could be done!

You, the reader, have had your own impossible dreams and foolish ideas. Maybe you have a vision now. I hope that in some way Leavenworth's story might encourage you to be willing to follow your own inspiration.

Bob Rodgers and I were newcomers to Leavenworth when we suggested a Bavarian theme as a way to revitalize the community and discussed new ideas to promote tourism as an industry. The response was to be expected:

"It won't work!"

"Where are you going to get the money for it?"

"You're not an expert—how do you expect to do that without professional know-how?"

"Why can't you leave things the way they are? Why do you have to change things?"

"We don't want any 'furiners' here from Seattle! No outsider is going to tell us what to do!"

"Why a German theme? We don't have a lot of Germans here."

"Tourism isn't an industry—we never made a nickel on a tourist yet!"

"You're just here to make a lot of money off of us!"

But those attitudes gradually changed and the town you see today reflects those changes. Its story begins with the spirit that lies within all of us—a spirit that, when awakened, can make miracles happen.

~

Getting To Know Leavenworth

"[Tumwater Canyon] is probably one of the most awe-inspiring canyons in the world—nine miles long and the mountain ranges on each side, some over a mile high!"

—Archie Marlin

"Leavenworth was never blessed with much money. It had had so much adversity. It's a town that was a boom and bust town for so many years....We'd fly high, then down it would go again."

—Pauline Watson

Leavenworth is located at the base of the eastern slopes of the Cascade Mountains, very near the geographical center of Washington. The town's elevation is about 1,100 feet, with mountains rising 5,000-8,000 feet nearby.

The earliest people known to inhabit the Leavenworth area were Native Americans, chiefly of the Yakama, Chinook and Wenatchi tribes. In the 1860s the Gold Rush brought white settlers into the region, and by 1890 home-steaders had spread along the upper Wenatchee River and Icicle Valley.

Early Boom Times

Leavenworth was in fact first called Icicle—an isolated little log-cabin town whose supplies had to be carried over the mountains by wagons and pack animals and whose river could only be crossed by boat or raft or forded during the late summer months. Before long, however, the Great Northern Railway Company began laying tracks up the valley along the route of today's Highway 2 and built a switchyard, assuring the town's importance in the region. Early in 1893 there were reportedly some 700 residents, and in April of

Scenes of early Leavenworth.
Opposite, top. Wooden buildings
before the turn of the century,
when disastrous fires struck.
Opposite, bottom. A bird's eye
view of Leavenworth ca. 1900,
with the Wenatchee River mill
pond visible (far upper right).

This page, clockwise from top
left. Lumberyard workers.
Construction of Leavenworth's
Wenatchee River Dam, creating
the mill pond. One of the many
trains that ran along what is now
Highway 2. Looking west toward
Tumwater Canyon and Front
Street. My partner, Bob Rodgers,
and I later bought the building
at the far left and remodeled it
in Old Bavarian style as the
Tannenbaum Building.

More scenes of early Leavenworth. Above. This corner building at Front Street and Ninth is now the Edelweiss Hotel. Below. Looking west down Front Street.

Opposite, top. Front Street. The two small wooden buildings (right) stand on the site of today's beautiful Downtown City Park, where visitors enjoy Art in the Park and bandstand concerts. Opposite, bottom. Front Street during early boom times, with "Tin Lizzies".

that year the present town site was platted by the Okanogan Investment Company and named for its president, Captain Charles Leavenworth.

In 1904 the Lamb-Davis Lumber Company built a large sawmill in Leavenworth, and twenty-nine lumber camps sprang up. Also in the early 1900s thousands of pear and apple trees were planted along the Icicle and upper Wenatchee River valleys. With the construction of miles of irrigation ditches, a successful fruit industry evolved, one that has largely survived to this day.

With this economic explosion, Leavenworth became a boomtown almost overnight and was dubbed "the wildest town in the West." Drinking and gambling went unchecked in thirteen saloons, and several brothels opened downtown—one of the largest in what is today the Tannenbaum Building on Front Street. Thus, long before Leavenworth became a Bavarian village, it prospered from the railroad, lumber and fruit industries and its population soared to some 5,500—more than nearby Wenatchee could claim! But almost as quickly as it blossomed, the economy of Leavenworth withered

MAIN STREET, LEAVENWORTH, WN.

9

and died. In the 1920s both the lumber and railroad industries turned off the lights and left town. With the crash of 1929, followed by the Great Depression of the 1930s, Leavenworth sank into economic ruin.

Those hard times continued through the 1940s and 1950s but in 1960, at Cole's Corner some fifteen miles away, Bob Rodgers and I bought a failing roadside restaurant and—inspired by the magnificent mountains that surrounded it—adopted an Alpine theme and Bavarian decor. Although we didn't know it then, this decision would later herald a new life for Leavenworth. The Squirrel Tree, as we called the restaurant, soon became a very popular attraction and we began to realize that a Bavarian theme might just be the answer to Leavenworth's economic woes.

Bob and I Get to Know the Leavenworth Valley

When Bob and I first went to Leavenworth, both of us had jobs that required traveling through the town regularly. We loved the wilderness surrounding the east slopes of the Cascades and were drawn to the area because we both enjoyed skiing, hiking, camping, fishing and being close to nature.

Bob was a Seattle native who was drafted in 1942 and served with General Patton's Third Army in France. When the war ended, he was assigned to the occupation forces in Munich, in the heart of Bavaria. Bob liked the Old World features of this region, particularly the distinctive architectural style of the buildings and houses, and he developed a great fondness for the culture of Bavaria.

The time he spent traveling around that part of southern Germany, studying the architecture, enjoying the arts and music, the food, the festivals, the folk dancing and the colorful attire, would later influence the revitalization of a small town in the States with the very un-Germanic name of Leavenworth!

Coming home, Bob enrolled at the University of Washington but soon decided the academic life was not for him. He took a job as an inspector for the State of Washington Department of Food and Drugs—a move that would benefit him later because it gave him some understanding of the restaurant business.

Me? Well, I am an Oregon boy, born in Portland in 1923, the youngest of three boys. My ancestry is quite mixed—Norwegian and English on my father's side and German, English and French on my mother's. Mother grew up in a beautiful house in downtown Portland (near where the Galleria Building stands today). Her father, Dr. Herbert C. Miller, founded the North Pacific School of Dentistry and Pharmacy in Portland. He subsequently donated the school to the state, and it became the University of Oregon School of Dentistry.

My parents divorced when I was in the third grade, and afterwards Mom raised us three boys in her gentle, loving way through the difficult years of the Depression.

My mother wasn't religious in the sense of being a church member; rather, she was very spiritual. She always stressed the importance of following our own hearts and taught us children how in the United States every person has the freedom to choose his own way. As a youngster I attended many different churches, which helped me to be open-minded and accepting of others.

I am forever grateful to my mother for encouraging me to discover my own spiritual direction and learn to follow this inner guidance. Her teaching gave me the key to living and, more than anything else, led to my vision of how Leavenworth might be transformed into a Bavarian village.

Sergeant Bob Rodgers (top row, right) with villagers in Dalem, France, 1944.

As a boy, I also loved animals and nature and spent my free time outdoors, roaming the forests, mountains, riverbanks and Oregon desert. I attended different schools in Portland and Sandy, where I finished grade school. In 1940, when I was a high school junior, however, adventure beckoned and I joined the U.S. Marine Corps Reserve. I wanted to get away from home and was eager to travel—especially to places with sunshine and palm trees!

Less than a month after I joined, my unit was called to active duty. When Pearl Harbor was attacked a year later, we were sent to Hawaii—in the first convoy to sail into the harbor after it was bombed. What a horrible sight that was—a devastated port filled with the remains of damaged and sunken ships.

From Hawaii I was sent to San Diego as a drill instructor and taught chemical warfare defense. I also attended a camouflage school at 20th Century Fox Studios in Beverly Hills, where we lived in tents right there on the studio grounds. I enjoyed this training, rose quickly in the ranks and soon became an instructor in camouflage. Someone said I might have been one of the youngest sergeants in the Marines.

When my unit received orders to ship out overseas, I was prevented from sailing with it by a new Navy ruling that required a one-year interval between

On furlough from the Marines, with my mother Hope Price at her home in Portland, Oregon. Mom always aspired to be a writer, and many of her short stories appeared in national publications. Later she wrote publicity releases promoting the natural beauty of the Leavenworth area.

overseas tours of duty. Since Hawaii was not yet a state, the Marine Corps considered my previous service there as foreign duty. I learned later that nearly every member of my unit sent to the South Pacific was killed in action.

Next, I was sent to Keyport, Washington, where I got into trouble one day using camouflage techniques to apply a simulated bullet hole to the forehead of a fellow marine. As he ran over to the barracks, laughing wildly, to show his buddy, other marines reacted in shock. Just as the general alarm for the base was about to be sounded, they rushed him into sick bay to treat the wound and give him a shot of morphine. When the hoax was discovered, the commanding officer told me, "You've taken ten years off my life tonight." As a result of my prank, I received a thirty-day restriction to the base!

From Keyport I was sent to the Aleutian Islands where, through correspondence school, I received my high school diploma. Finally, I was sent to Camp Pendleton near San Diego until the end of the war. The happiest day of my life in the service was the day I received an honorable discharge and headed home!

I never cared much for school, but nevertheless, when I returned I enrolled at Oregon State University to study engineering—for a while. Then I studied geology and photography, but I really didn't know what I wanted to do to earn a living. When I finally took an aptitude test, the results showed that, above all else, I should not pursue chemistry. However, my best friend had just chosen pharmacy as his major, so in spite of the aptitude test I took the challenge, entered the School of Pharmacy and graduated in 1949.

For three years I was a practicing pharmacist in Portland and Seattle. Then I became a representative for Pfizer Laboratories and in that work covered northern Washington from Seattle to the Canadian border, east and west of the Cascade Mountains. This job took me frequently through central Washington and the Leavenworth area, primarily on business calls to doctors and druggists.

In those days, work wasn't everything: I still liked to play—especially to ski. I had belonged to the Oregon State University Mountain Club, and later I joined the ski patrols at Mt. Hood and at Santiam Pass.

I was happy with my life. I believed in the healing medicines I brought to people, the antibiotics and other drugs that promised to cure more and more diseases and ailments. Moreover, I was lucky enough to work in the most beautiful countryside imaginable! And I was driving all the time, which satisfied my somewhat restless nature. Truly, it was a full and exciting life.

Then in the mid-1950s, something happened that was to change my life forever: I was making a call in Anacortes, Washington, when I became extremely ill with jaundice. Up to then I had always been healthy. Now, for the first time, I was in the hospital, where my symptoms worsened so much that it appeared my condition might be terminal.

Afraid of dying, I did much soul searching. At times I blamed myself for the illness, wondering what I had done or failed to do that had brought me, at about age thirty, to the end of my life. Along with the fear, I felt empty and completely alone. Once I ran away from the hospital, then returned, despondent and with little hope for recovery.

During this time my mother attended me. She frequently spoke about the power of prayer, even though I was skeptical and resisted her religious messages. I now know that it was mostly through my mother that my health returned and, along with it, a whole new life. At the time, she greatly influ-

Talking to friends on the slopes at Timberline Lodge, Mt. Hood, Oregon, during my ski patrol days.

enced me to make a commitment to live spiritually, especially by the principles and practices taught by Jesus in the New Testament. My mother never joined a church, but she was most strongly drawn to the Unity and Infinite Way teachings, as I was in the years that followed my ordeal.

I felt I had been given a precious gift. With my recovery I adopted a completely different attitude toward myself, other people and the kind of life I wanted to lead. Little did I suspect that radical changes were soon to appear or that the next forty years would be so challenging and rewarding! Certainly I had no idea that my destiny was to be worked out in Leavenworth.

Merritt Inn

Shortly after my recovery I met Bob Rodgers. We became good friends as we discovered a mutual distaste for city life and love for the outdoors, particularly for fishing and skiing and for the mountains of central Washington. To explore the Northwest further, I took flying lessons and bought a small plane in which Bob and I explored Oregon, Washington and British Columbia. We especially enjoyed our trips to Vancouver Island, where we fished for Tyee, the large Chinook salmon.

In 1957 Bob and I rented a cabin at Merritt Inn, about twenty miles from Leavenworth on Highway 2 and close to Stevens Pass, where we liked to ski. One night shortly after we arrived there following a hard work week, I accidently set myself on fire. It was a bitterly cold evening and I was chilled to the bone. To warm up in a hurry, I lit all the burners on the kitchen stove and stood with my back to it.

Suddenly, my flannel pajamas caught fire and I was aflame. In a panic, I yelled and began to run. The fire quickly burned through my clothes, and I know I would have burned to death had Bob not heard my shouts, run into the room, thrown me to the floor and rolled the rug around me. Then he rushed me to the Leavenworth hospital, where they told me I might be scarred for life. Fortunately—and thanks largely to Bob's quick thinking— I recovered quickly without any trace of scars and we were able to go on spending our free time at our Merritt Inn cabin.

In those days, Merritt Inn was on a desolate stretch of Highway 2. On winter nights a traveler might see nothing for miles except six-foot high banks of snow lining both sides of the road. That isolation bothered some travelers, and for a couple of winters Bob and I tried to do some-

Inside the log cabin home of Otis (standing) and Millie Marsh, owners of Merritt Inn.

Me with my Cessna 140 in 1957, on one of the many fishing trips Bob Rodgers and I took around the Pacific Northwest.

thing special at Christmastime by decorating the Inn with hundreds of Christmas lights strung over the lodge, cabins and trees. For residents and motorists alike, the bright, warm Christmas lights were a welcome sight.

When winter ended, we decided to spend even more of our free time at the cabin. During the warmer months we fished the lakes and rivers and hiked in the mountains, and we took photographs year round. Both of us wanted to move out of the city, live in this great outdoors and somehow find a way to support ourselves, but we weren't sure we were willing to leave good jobs to do whatever was necessary to survive in the mountains. One answer might be to buy Merritt Inn. Otis and Millie Marsh, the elderly couple who owned it, wanted us to buy it from them and for a time we seriously considered their offer, but we ultimately decided simply to buy a cabin somewhere nearby. In later years, Merritt Inn was destroyed in a fire.

The Cole's Corner Cafe

One day, as we were searching for a cabin to buy, we stopped at the Cole's Corner Cafe, a roadside restaurant near Leavenworth at the junction of Highway 2 and the Lake Wenatchee Road. When we asked the owner, Ward Harris, about a cabin, he replied that the only thing for sale around there was his cafe and promptly quoted us a price. We certainly were not looking for a restaurant to buy, so we thanked him and left—after wolfing down generous servings of Mrs. Harris's homemade pies!

Cole's Corner Cafe in 1959 while we were still negotiating to buy it from Ward Harris. Our talks broke off until Christmas, when Ward sent us a note saying, "I'm ready to make with the talk." We remodeled the restaurant in Bavarian style and renamed it The Squirrel Tree.

By this time, we had fallen in love with the Leavenworth area—and with Mrs. Harris's delicious pies—so we made many return visits to the Cole's Corner Cafe. Every time we saw Ward Harris, he hounded us to buy the restaurant, and each time he lowered his sale price. What he didn't tell us was the fact that the restaurant was nearly bankrupt and everything was about to be repossessed.

As time passed and we seemed to have no luck finding a cabin, we began to seriously consider Ward's offer. We talked to our friends and some "experts" about it, and everybody warned us against the idea. Even my dad, who had been in the restaurant business himself, said, "Don't be foolish, Ted! Don't be stupid!"

There was one exception, however—George McBrian, a friend and restaurant owner in Portland. George was a Christian Scientist who always looked on the bright side of life. His advice was, "Well, you know you guys are so naive, you can't fail! You'll be all right. Don't worry about it."

So early in 1960, armed with our naivety, a total lack of experience, just enough cash and a ton of enthusiasm, we took the step that was to change both of our lives forever.

~ 3 ~

The Origin of
the Bavarian Theme

*"My ideas would have gone nowhere had Ted not taken hold of them
and been able to see what could happen. Because he's a visionary and
I'm more for what's happening today. A person can have ideas but if
they're not put to use, well, they don't get anywhere."*

— *Bob Rodgers*

*"It was good food. Their business was terrific! Our daughter Donna
worked there for a while, and she said, 'I've never seen anything like
it! People just come and come and come!'"*

— *Vi Rembold*

Almost as soon as we bought the Cole's Corner Cafe, Bob quit his job,
moved into the restaurant and began getting everything ready to reopen.
We wanted a new name for our establishment, and after considering different
possibilities settled on "The Squirrel Tree." As we considered how to make
our restaurant the very best place in the area for good food and a good time,
we also decided to adopt a theme. But what theme? Whatever we chose, we
wanted to carry it out in an authentic manner.

The Bavarian Motif Is Introduced

My preference was a Native American motif, but Bob talked of introducing the Swiss Bavarian one he had encountered in Europe after the war. He
had returned there in 1955 and taken many photographs of the scenery, architecture, flowers and decorative elements. Now, as we looked at his photographs, we began to see how we could adopt many of the same effects at The
Squirrel Tree. And of course we were well aware of how closely the mountains

and valleys and trees of our region resembled those found in the Alpine country of Europe.

That was it! We decided to go all out with Bob's idea. The Alpine theme would prevail in our restaurant. However, we were still unsure what to call it. It was definitely Alpine, but was it also Swiss? Was it Bavarian? Most often we called it Swiss Bavarian.

From the beginning we set a high standard for authenticity. We hired Baroness Margaret von Wrangel, a talented artist, to paint a large mural of an Alpine mountain climber outside on the great fireplace wall. She also painted flowers, birds, small animals, bells and other figures on the roof scalloping, gable, trimboards, shutters and window boxes.

On April 9, 1960, The Squirrel Tree opened its doors and, to our joy and amazement, the restaurant was an immediate success. In that first year, after covering remodeling costs, improvements and expenses, we showed a net profit of $201!

As Bob said, "We were not really restaurant people. The only thing we knew about a restaurant was being a customer and what customers liked!" This attitude determined the menus we prepared:

Top right. Inside The Squirrel Tree a balcony featured large dolls in Bavarian attire above a sign announcing the first Washington State Autumn Leaf Festival (1964). Bottom right. Waitresses wore homemade dirndls. Left. Baroness Margaret von Wrangel paints an Alpine mountaineer mural on the outdoor fireplace chimney.

"These young gentlemen came into the area. They bought The Squirrel Tree, and I think really that was the start of many things. They did so much work on the building and made it Swiss — even the waitresses were in dirndls. The balcony overlooking the main restaurant — there were figures of little boys and girls in dirndls and lederhosen. They put (out) colorful flowers. . .did a lot of landscaping. And then the gentlemen, the boys, built that beautiful motel in the same motif. And it was a going concern!

— Wilfred Davy

we kept the food plain American because, frankly, we didn't know how to make Swiss or Bavarian food well. However, we bought only the best ingredients and from the beginning we had regular deliveries of high-grade meat from Bothell and Wenatchee. Also, we placed daily orders for special breads and buns from a bakery in Everett. (Later the baking was done in Leavenworth.)

All the waitresses wore homemade dirndls, the native Bavarian dress. During mealtimes we played Swiss and German oom-pah-pah music, most of which included yodeling, often to the dismay of our waitresses! We worked hard to create a holiday atmosphere. Bob recalls:

> There were lines of people waiting to get in, and most people thought we were making money hand over fist. It was coming in really well. But it's not what you take in—it's what you keep—and it was going out faster than it came in! There was more red ink on the ledger than there was black.

Soon, in the front of the restaurant we opened a souvenir and gift shop with imported merchandise. In June of 1960, while attending a gift show in Los Angeles to acquire merchandise for our shop, we stopped at Knott's Berry Farm and asked if we could talk to the owner, Walter Knott. To our surprise, he kindly invited us in for a good hour's talk and gave us excellent suggestions for running a successful restaurant.

Our Forest Friends—
The Bears and Other Wildlife

Tourists and locals weren't our only visitors at The Squirrel Tree; we encouraged wildlife to visit the grounds to put on their own show. It was quite a spectacle—squirrels, deer, wild bears, even coyotes. The bears and squirrels, especially, would come during the day for handouts.

Our excellent head cook, Penny Ells, made quite a name for herself by befriending Old Gorgeous George, a seven-foot tall black bear that frequented the restaurant to enjoy the pastries and maple bars Penny fed him—sometimes from her own mouth! Old George and as many as fifteen of his companions would come down from the woods to eat and play and chase one another around outside the restaurant. Our customers were de-

20

"But the interesting thing about the tourist attraction was not only the squirrels, and the beautiful flowers they had there, but the bears....They were wild bears! They came right up to the window so the tourists could watch them! They'd wrestle! The bears would wrestle each other!"

— Walt Rembold

BEWARE
DO NOT APPROACH
WILD BEARS
THE
Squirrel
Tree

"That's me and my darned ole piggy Gorgeous George, my favorite bear at The Squirrel Tree, about 1962. I used to feed him outside the forest by throwing food to him, but he got so he came in close to the restaurant.

When one of my bosses said, 'He's tame for the fellow up at the Ox Bow—he feeds him out of his hand!' I said, 'Well, if a man can do it, I can!' And he said, 'Aren't you afraid?' And I said, 'No! I was raised on a farm.' So I got candy bars and I went out.

It took three weeks to get him up to this point—where I could feed him out of my hand. And he got real tame. He was real nice. You see, when he takes those out of my mouth, he's so careful. He doesn't dare bite the face that feeds him, or he wouldn't get any more food!

I worked up there eight years at The Squirrel Tree and fed Old George every year."

—Penny Ells

lighted, but one day these antics attracted the attention of an employee of the Fish and Game Department, who warned us about having the bears so close to the restaurant. This so annoyed Bob that he invited the man to leave.

On the porch at The Squirrel Tree we hung a picture board that showed the entire area and the special features of each season: fishing in the spring, the bears and the lake area in the summer and autumn leaves in the fall. We did not promote hunting. Bob and I share a deep regard for the sanctity of all life, so we did everything we could to care for and protect the animals in the

Above. Tiny's place in Cashmere, Washington (11 miles east of Leavenworth). Tiny (right) and his partner Dean Slechta (left) turned their fruit stand into a showplace and inspired us to expand our own use of flowers at The Squirrel Tree and Chalet Motel.

Opposite. An artist's conception of our restaurant and motel, 1961.

area. When hunters asked where the best hunting was, we sent them off on a wild goose chase.

Flowers and Autumn Leaves

Every year we planted a galaxy of flowers. And here we must give credit to Dick "Tiny" Graves. Tiny was well known in the region for his impressive fruit stand in Cashmere, a small town about eleven miles from Leavenworth. His stand was always overflowing with thousands of flowers.

Whenever I visited Tiny in Cashmere, he always wanted to go inside his giant walk-in refrigerator to talk—he was cooler and more comfortable there! Sometimes Tiny and his business associate Dean Slechta ate at The Squirrel Tree, where Tiny frequently dined on two top sirloin steaks!

Tiny spoke with gusto when he was enthusiastic about something, and one day when I asked him what more we could do to beautify the restaurant and attract customers, he gave me a great suggestion: "Everything is perfect except for one thing," he said excitedly, "you need a lot more flowers! And I'd put them alongside the highway where everybody can enjoy them. It would really set this place off!"

We already had a variety of wild and domestic flowers, including beds of snapdragons and window boxes and hanging baskets spilling over with fuchsias, petunias and other blossoms. Nevertheless, we took Tiny's advice and planted new beds, including a petunia bed over 100 feet long beside the highway. In the spring we featured displays of mock orange and other wildflowers.

There were drawbacks to Tiny's plan, however. We lacked a plentiful water supply. (All we had was a well, and a nearby creek that dried up during the summer.) We also had problems with the ground squirrels and chipmunks, who enjoyed eating the flowers, and the bears, who loved to romp in the beds. And often the hanging flower baskets were buffeted by strong mountain winds which made confetti out of the fuchsia blossoms.

Besides the flowers, we liked to decorate our establishment with leaves. The fall foliage in the mountains and valleys is truly spectacular, so when the vine maples began to turn color we used them to decorate the restaurant. To encourage more travelers to the area, we also sent press releases to regional newspapers and radio stations and my mother wrote articles with glowing tributes to the autumn leaves.

Each fall we kept a daily record of temperatures and weather conditions so that we could more accurately predict when the leaves would start turning the following year. Our annual autumn leaf publicity efforts evolved over the years, and later I introduced the idea of a special autumn leaf celebration in Leavenworth. That led to Leavenworth's originating the Washington State Autumn Leaf Festival, one of the major annual events in the state.

Dreams of a Bavarian Village

I know today that Bob and I were drawn to Leavenworth for more than just our own business success and personal well being. Somehow, in the way

"I couldn't visualize all the things that Ted was talking about. And when you say talk, I mean it went on for hours and days and weeks and months! We explored the various avenues that would at that time increase our business and be kind of a fun thing to do. Really, neither one of us was just interested in operating another restaurant per se. When we started the theme, we kept adding to it and adding to it, as new ideas came to us."
— Bob Rodgers

This page. My partner Bob Rodgers removes snow from the roof of our motel. Because we were at a higher elevation than Leavenworth, our winters were more severe and we had to deal with deeper snows. Here Bob uses a crosscut saw to separate the snow into large blocks before sliding them off the roof with a shovel.

Opposite, top. Details of Old Bavarian design include a large overhanging roof with painted corbels, perpendicular balcony boards with cutouts and scalloped bargeboards with artwork along the roof edge and below the balcony. Opposite, bottom. From left, Bob Rodgers, our good friend Carolyn Schutte, and me with Carolyn's guests, Ken and Florence Wolford.

we ran The Squirrel Tree, we brought enjoyment to others—people who lived in the Leavenworth area as well as travelers. This in turn performed a service to the community.

As soon as I realized how much people liked coming to The Squirrel Tree, I wondered about developing other businesses with this same Alpine theme. There were countless times when sitting alone at night or driving along the local roads, I let my imagination roam. Daydreaming? Fantasizing? Meditating? I couldn't say, but my mind was filled with ideas and plans for new projects. In time, I came to trust this practice more and more.

One idea I had was a colossal one: why not build an entire Old World village right there at Cole's Corner? The first step of course would be to obtain the land, so in 1961, within a year of opening The Squirrel Tree, we purchased a parcel of land of roughly ten acres, including two more of the "corners" at our crossroads.

We ourselves drew up the basic plans for the new village, with all the designs in the Swiss Bavarian architectural style. Where our restaurant and a neighbor's gas station stood, I imagined a cluster of buildings. Our plans also included creating a small reflection lake along the highway to Lake Wenatchee, behind which old Bavarian-style shops and other buildings would rise, reflected in the lake's waters from the light of Old European street lamps that would ring its shores.

Our venture was thwarted in 1963 when we tried to acquire eighty more acres at Cole's Corner and the owner decided at the last minute not to sell. This setback didn't stop my dreaming, though. Instead, it forced me to realize my vision elsewhere, maybe to create a theme town in nearby Leavenworth.

The Squirrel Tree Chalet Motel

Meanwhile, due to travelers' requests for lodging and strong suggestions from a few good friends, we built the first Bavarian-style motel in the state—The Squirrel Tree Chalet Motel. Bob and I drew up a rough design featuring a big overhanging roof. Of course we were not experienced at managing a motel, either, so we were again risking everything on this project. Our open house was

"Actually, that [Squirrel Tree] was a forerunner of what happened in Leavenworth. And I think that's what gave Ted the idea about starting the same thing in Leavenworth, because they were very successful up there. It was fantastic! I mean, I've never seen any architecture like that! But it looked beautiful and attracted the tourists."

— Walt Rembold

NEW MOTEL—A new motel is contemplated on Stevens Pass highway by Ted Price and Bob Rodgers. Here is an artist's conception of the structure.

Swiss Alps' Chalet Motel Planned On Stevens Pass

LAKE WENATCHEE — The Swiss Alps will come to the Lake Wenatchee area in greater measure with the construction of a new motel on Steven's Pass Highway at Cole's Corner.

The motel is an expansion program of the Squirrel Tree Restaurant, owned by Ted Price and Bob Rodgers. The owners announce the motel, which will be pine exterior but a modern interior with wall-to-wall carpeting, electric heat and a Hi Fi.

Construction is to begin immediately so the first six units can be completed by April 1.

Art work on the new motel will be done by Baroness Margaret Von Wrangel, of Seattle formerly of Estonia, the owners said. The architect is Donald Avery, Olym-

held December 1, 1961. While we were still considering our plans for expansion and new developments, an event of international importance was about to begin in Seattle, some 100 miles to the west of Leavenworth.

The Enchanted Land—
U.S. Highway 2: From Everett to Spokane

In 1962 the Seattle World's Fair opened, and motorists arriving from all directions promised to create boom times for towns throughout the area. To attract World's Fair visitors traveling on Highway 2, we spent a large amount of our Squirrel Tree advertising budget on signs, radio and newspaper features and other advertising, including flyers and postcards. In addition, we leased billboard space and built more highway signs. In every way we could, we promoted local vacation possibilities, the autumn leaves, sporting activities and of course The Squirrel Tree Restaurant and Chalet Motel.

We were alarmed, though, to discover that very few people used Highway 2 as a route to the World's Fair.

Soon, Bob and I decided to do something about this. We knew that future efforts to publicize our restaurant and motel had to include Leavenworth and all the other communities along Highway 2. This meant pooling our advertising funds with businesses in other towns. Accordingly, we drove across Washington on Highway 2, at our own expense, and stopped in almost every town along the way to talk with people, including members of the chambers of commerce and various business groups. Before each visit, we phoned or sent letters to chamber or business association heads so that a meeting could be scheduled. Often, when we arrived in a town we found a large number of merchants eagerly awaiting these special meetings. Over the months, we made many trips back and forth across the state, trying to convince everyone of the necessity for cooperative publicity efforts.

At that time, billboards along the highway were in common use, but to my way of thinking the regulations governing them were too restrictive. This perception spurred Bob and me into action to amend the 1961 State Scenic Highway Billboard Act—a new law prohibiting private signs along the highway.

How wrong-headed I was! While campaigning for this amendment, I met Marjorie Phillips of the Washington State Arts Commission, who convinced me that small signs benefitted everyone and that large billboards led only to larger billboards and more highway eyesores! Doing a complete turn-around, I joined with others in a zealous campaign to pass even more restrictive highway sign control measures—fewer and smaller signs, and signs harmonious to the environment. (Later, when engaged in the revitalization of Leavenworth, Bob and I championed sign standards and control as key factors in creating an Old World look.)

As I worked in the early 1960s to bring more business into the Leavenworth and Lake Wenatchee areas, tourism loomed larger and larger in my thoughts. An important step at this time was joining the Stevens Pass Association, which we later renamed the U.S. Highway 2 Association. Through this body we launched a cooperative advertising campaign to promote tourism along the entire highway in Washington state, from Everett to Spokane.

For this campaign a major publicity piece was needed, so we urged individuals in each community to write about local activities and tourist attractions. Along with these articles, we collected beautiful scenic photographs of the region, some of which I took. Even then, we wanted Leavenworth to be a tourist destination rather than just a stop along the way to somewhere else.

We took our materials to Franklin Press in Yakima, which published the *Washington State Travel Book*, and Franklin agreed to publish *U.S. Highway 2 and North: The Enchanted Land*, a full-color illustrated booklet that would sell for fifty cents. Later, our booklet was to become an addition to the *Travel Book*.

Among the many benefits we derived from this enterprise was the opportunity to meet new people in business and government. Moreover, the project's success made me even more convinced that tourism, as an industry, could save the economy of Leavenworth. Everywhere we went we received strong support and encouragement from the business people, but we received more financial support from the business community of Leavenworth than from any other town—especially from the owners of restaurants, service stations and motels. These merchants were also enthusiastic about developing tourism as an industry for their town.

At the end of the 1962 tourist season, the publisher of the *Waterville Empire Press*, Howard Ordway, gave us a nice pat on the back in the November 29 issue of his newspaper:

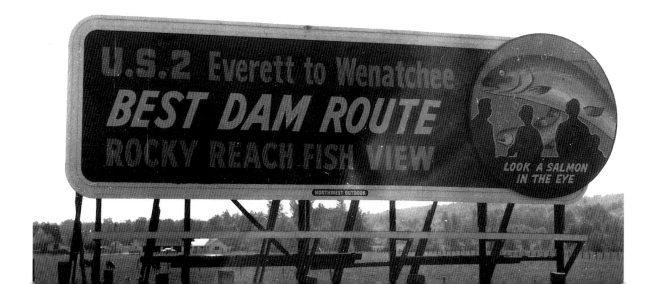

Price and Rodgers were the two men most responsible for our excellent tourist business this year. It didn't just happen....It took time, organization and selfless work to do the job. Price and Rodgers have a most interesting program that will help every business in town, especially the motels, service stations, restaurants, and local firms who meet the tourists. Their ideas will be worth money to the community next spring and summer.

Leavenworth in 1960

We had come to know well the depth of Leavenworth's economic condition. Progress had passed it by. It was even dubbed a welfare town. One by one, businesses were closing, leaving empty storefronts and buildings in disrepair. As LaVerne Peterson recalls, "We were just existing, is all we were. [My restaurant business] was just the local trade...the people were going past, but they weren't stopping." And for many young people like Jack Dorsey, Leavenworth was a good place to be from. As Jack tells it, "I hate to say this, but [the principal] told me in the men's lavatory at high school, 'Jack, get the h-e-l-l out....There is no future in Leavenworth!'"

In those days, very little merchandise remained on the shelves of Leavenworth's stores and townspeople were beginning to shop in nearby towns. Also, a major problem was tearing the community apart: the state of Washington had condemned Leavenworth High School and for several years the people had been embroiled in a controversy over the choice of a site on which to build a new school. With the entire community divided into various warring factions, it was a sad and ugly conflict. Some neighbors would not speak to one another and established friendships were threatened.

Vera Lee of *The Leavenworth Echo* remembers her frustration: "The town was just split open, and I would have moved, except I wouldn't have been able to sell my home and my business. So we were pretty much forced to stay."

Crippled with this problem, along with the longstanding effects of a depressed economy, Leavenworth was desperate for solutions. Relief and assistance came in the form of a self-help program that was to see Leavenworth rise once more, like the Phoenix, from its own ashes.

At the same time, events in Leavenworth were drawing us into a deeper commitment to the town's survival. Yet as newcomers and owners of a popular restaurant, we didn't have a sense of desperation about the town's economic plight. On the contrary, the more I looked to Leavenworth, the more I began to see it becoming the prosperous Bavarian village I'd first imagined creating at Cole's Corner. I dared to wonder if we could convince the townspeople to remodel their dying town in that style. Even if they could afford it, would the merchants be willing to risk the expense of remodeling and do so with no guarantee of any success whatsoever? Most importantly, would they listen to us "big-city" outsiders, whose only local credentials were The Squirrel Tree Restaurant and Chalet Motel?

It seemed clear that Bob and I would need to take the first step, to buy property in downtown Leavenworth and start remodeling ourselves. Perhaps other business people would follow.

~ 4 ~

A Vision of
Bavarian Leavenworth

"Well, there isn't any question about that in my mind—Ted Price and Bob Rodgers are the ones that started the whole Bavarian theme here."
—Bob Johnson

"Our visit to Solvang, California gave us the idea that, instead of starting from scratch, with having to put in sewers and water, and all the facilities and streets—that would cost a fortune...why not concentrate on this town that was about fifteen miles from us that was decayed?"

— Bob Rodgers

In some ways, Leavenworth turned out to be a better site than Cole's Corner for creating a Bavarian village. In Leavenworth, we wouldn't have to erect new buildings or install sewer or water facilities, as we would have had to do at Cole's Corner.

And what a beautiful town it would be, spreading out at the foot of spectacular mountains with the crystal-clear Wenatchee River flowing almost through its center. Truly, you couldn't find a more ideal setting for a Bavarian village!

Yet in those days Leavenworth itself was scarcely beautiful. Conditions were bad and likely to get worse. Many buildings were empty, many already boarded up. The town was obviously dying. And yet for that very reason, maybe—just maybe—the townspeople would be open to new ideas and willing to explore the possibility of transforming their town, not just superficially, but in an authentic, comprehensive way.

The vision I had then for Leavenworth included:

1. Bavarian architecture with exterior walls of stucco and timber; large over-hanging roofs (8 feet or more) with scalloped trim; traditional Bavarian colors on all signs, artwork and trim; exterior wall murals depicting mountains and village life; balconies, with quaint cutouts on perpendicular boards and Bavarian trim; shutters, also with cutout designs and flowers everywhere—on the balconies, window boxes, sidewalk hanging baskets and in other plantings.

2. A town glockenspiel.

3. Bell towers.

4. Lively Bavarian music, with yodeling and oom-pah-pah, the zither and the accordion.

5. Dancing—especially the Schuhplattler and other folk dances performed in peasant costume—dirndles for the women and lederhosen for the men.

6. A downtown "walking town" with a very tight core area oriented to the Wenatchee River and the mountain views, unobtrusive parking lots, no mini-malls and very clean streets and sidewalks.

7. Parks and promenades along the river with an Old World covered bridge to Blackbird Island.

8. An emphasis on the arts.

34

"When I came into Leavenworth, I came in a brand new 1956 Ford sedan, and it had a Thunderbird engine. We parked outside the city hall. I was sitting there, waiting for my dad to conduct some business, when Slim Hollingsworth brought his mule train pack animals down the main street. And he parked right out in front of city hall—right next to our car! I thought I was out in the wild west."

— Jack Dorsey

9. Art shows held outdoors in the downtown parks.

10. A genuine European bakery, with a large, round communal table where the townspeople could gather, discuss ideas and enjoy people-watching.

11. Old World street lamps, adorned with flower baskets and Old European light fixtures on businesses.

12. Small outdoor signs for business names—like those of Old Bavaria.

13. A European bandstand in the downtown park, surrounded by flowers and adorned with hanging flower baskets.

14. Lively festivals and special celebrations throughout the year emphasizing all the seasons: a German-type spring festival, an autumn festival focusing on the colorful vine maple and aspen leaves, a Christmastime display featuring thousands of lights.

15. Large road signs in German at the town's center, as well as other signs along the highway approaching town—with the distances given in kilometers rather than miles.

16. The slogan "A Bavarian Village" and perhaps a change in the name of Leavenworth to an appropriate-sounding Alpine one.

17. A focus on a town largely free of crime.

18. A town that would not have a carnival atmosphere, which meant not having beer festivals.

19. Remodeling done as authentically as possible, because this would generate free publicity and this is what would truly distinguish Leavenworth.

Visitors would be able to enjoy Leavenworth free of charge.

Project LIFE—Leavenworth Improvement for Everyone

Project LIFE proved to be the first major step toward economic health and a new sense of unity for the people of Leavenworth. In 1962 the Chamber of Commerce called on the Bureau of Community Development at the University of Washington, which had helped other communities. In response, the Bureau provided Leavenworth with a self-study program whereby the townspeople could find their own solutions to their problems. They would not be told what to do, only how to work together and how to find special resource people who could help.

The first meeting was in October 1962, when the people unanimously approved a name for the project that had been suggested by Joan James: "L.I.F.E.—Leavenworth Improvement For Everyone." Joan was a member of the Vesta Junior Women's Club, a very active organization dedicated to helping the town. The Chairman of Project LIFE was the esteemed former mayor, Bob Brender. Bob had served on the Leavenworth City Council two or three terms and then as mayor for two terms.

Project LIFE was an ambitious, long-term, self-help project that studied not only Leavenworth but the surrounding area—in essence, every element of life in the Upper Wenatchee Valley. The project committees numbered fifteen and included education, planning, churches, libraries, youth, agriculture, trades and services, beautification, labor and industry and parks and recreation. (Unfortunately, a tourist committee was not at first proposed.) At its completion, some two and one-half years later,

this self-examination project was deemed the most successful of all those supervised by the University of Washington. Ken Nyberg, community consultant at the university, said:

> Leavenworth has a sense of community, not place. There are numerous examples of towns in Eastern Washington with similar histories that died. Leavenworth had a strong sense of built-in preservation.

One purpose of the study was to determine if three current sources of income—logging, agriculture and, to a lesser extent, tourism—could be expanded and new industries brought in.

Because the school issue was so explosive, all committees were told to avoid controversy or any discussion of this problem. Rather, people were urged to work positively on projects.

Because they had a common goal, the townspeople's enthusiasm soon became evident, as did their earlier spirit of cooperation and volunteerism. Soon, 200 of the town's nearly 1,500 people were working on the various committees and Project LIFE became a turning point for the entire population. In that regard, Bob Brender's statement about the urgency and goals of Project LIFE was prophetic:

> "We must develop from the study a sound plan for community action. It is necessary for full development of the community's resources, and to create that spirit of unity and citizen alertness which is needed to make the action program a permanent, ongoing success...and above all, we must act to assure the continued health, safety, general welfare and spiritual life of all our people."

Despite the promise Project LIFE held, however, I was disturbed by the omission of a tourism committee. The University of Washington consultant, Dirk Anderson, indicated that the Bureau of Community Development had never before authorized a tourism committee, but after my persistent requests he relented and said if I would serve as chair he would create such a committee. I readily agreed.

As chairman of the newly installed LIFE Tourism Committee, I repeatedly brought up the idea of tourism as an economy. It seemed impractical to develop agriculture or logging industries then, so I proposed that Leavenworth become a theme town. I also suggested we inaugurate an annual autumn leaf festival as a special publicity event to bring more visitors and new businesses to Leavenworth.

"Project LIFE...could well be one of the greatest events ever to happen to this community in promoting understanding and trust, developing cooperation, creating a knowledge of your home area's assets and failings, and of the part your friend and neighbor plays in its progress, either as an individual or as a member of one of the many organizations.

No one should feel excluded in this program. There's a part for everyone if he wants it. It is a project that will require several months to complete, and there are numerous committees which will require many members. No one will be overtaxed, and in this manner it will truly be a community-wide endeavor."

—Russell D. Lee, Publisher, The Leavenworth Echo

Opposite. The story on the Vesta Junior Women's Club which ran in The Seattle Sunday Times *on September 20, 1964. The Vesta Junior Women's Club was the first Washington state club ever to win the Sears Award. The award was given in recognition of the group's outstanding community services in the LIFE program, and for its role in securing a levy for a new fire hall and fire truck, helping to resolve the bitter school site dispute, maintaining a cemetery beautification project and cleaning up and landscaping the Downtown City Park.*

Regrettably, there was little enthusiasm for the idea of developing a theme at this time, particularly an Alpine theme. While there was genuine interest among some committee members, others were not so enthusiastic. One member chided me, saying, "You wouldn't want the town of Leavenworth to take the same theme as you have at The Squirrel Tree, would you?" Many of the committee members were from the Lake Wenatchee area. For them, to develop tourism meant to improve sporting and recreational facilities in the area (especially the bridle trails), stock Fish Lake with trout and create view points at scenic spots along the highway.

As the idea of changing the architecture of Leavenworth grew in my imagination, however, I asked committee member Walt Rembold, a high school science and math teacher and a photographer, to take pictures of each downtown building. Most committee members said that such a step was expensive and unnecessary, but Walt agreed to do it for me personally at cost. I paid Walt's expenses for this job, because it seemed very important that if the people did agree to remodel, there be a photographic record of the town for historical purposes.

Walt said, "I don't know why Ted had this foresight, but he had me take pictures of every building in town. I couldn't see why in the world he wanted pictures of those dilapidated buildings. But he was very precise in having the pictures taken—every building from the same angle—and Ted didn't miss a one. And I'll tell you, I took a lot of pictures!"

The most important meeting of the Tourism Committee was held June 15, 1964 at the Pine River Dude Ranch. We invited people from other Project LIFE committees, hoping to stimulate their interest and support for the autumn leaf festival as well as for the Alpine theme.

The meeting was a heated one, but finally an autumn leaf festival was approved. The chambers of commerce for Leavenworth and Lake Wenatchee were to work together to inaugurate the festival. Most importantly—the consensus at the meeting was that it would be feasible to remodel Leavenworth as an Alpine theme town and thereby develop tourism as an economy. Before this agreement was reached, however, some strong personal criticism of me was voiced, as were several objections to my proposals.

Among the guests at this meeting was Shirley Bowen, chairperson of the LIFE Trades and Services Committee. Shirley was also president of the Vesta Junior Women's Club, which had just won the Sears-Roebuck Foundation

How 11 Women Made Life Exciting

By ELIZABETH WRIGHT EVANS

HOW 11 young matrons, total membership of the Vesta Junior Women's Club, put the "leaven" in Leavenworth and thereby caused a ferment that saved their small town is a story that will bring to the town its most exciting event next Saturday.

The women won for their community the $10,000 prize of the Sears, Roebuck Foundation and the General Federation of Women's Clubs. It will be presented by the foundation president, James T. Griffin of Chicago, at 3:30 o'clock Saturday afternoon in Leavenworth as part of a week-long celebration titled the Washington State Autumn Festival.

To see the women get their award and to learn how they will spend it for their community, the town has invited every interested person and has planned a variety of other events. Principal among them will be bus tours to the surrounding hills to see the autumn leaves in their blazing glory.

There will be an all-day carnival Saturday, performances of a Gay 90's musical at 8 o'clock Thursday, Friday and Saturday, fish derbies and boat shows at Lake Wenatchee and a festival dance Saturday evening.

Bus tours from Seattle will leave the Seattle Center Coliseum at 8 o'clock in the morning Saturday and Sunday, returning from Leavenworth at 6 o'clock in the evening.

THE VESTA CLUB is the only junior club in the federation ever to win a national award in the competition, held every two years since 1955. Junior Clubs are those with members between 18 and 35 years.

The General Federation has more than 15,000 clubs throughout the country. In the first year 3,032 clubs entered; this year there were 9,976. Sears, Roebuck Foundation officials say the quality of the community service greatly improved over the years making it even more surprising that the tiny group of young women in Leavenworth could win.

No Washington State club ever has won before. When the Vesta members first heard that they had placed among the first ten clubs in the nation they began to feel the first flush of reward for several years of effort—all of it performed without help from baby-sitters. The women, among them, have 46 children; on many projects, the youngsters simply went along with their mothers.

And when, in June, at the national convention of the General Federation in Atlantic City, it was announced that the Vesta representative, Mrs. Charles Bowen, would take home with her the top award, the entire small town began, for the first time, really to appreciate how these determined young matrons had halted Leavenworth's stagnation.

In 1962, Vestas finally convinced their fellow townspeople that a community study, undertaken with the assistance of the University of Washington Bureau of Community Development, might solve some of their worst problems.

After failing three times to muster enough of the citizenry to meetings for consideration of a study, Vesta members finally went door to door, appointed some committees and held a final meeting in January, 1963, to which 250 persons came and the study got under way. Charmed Land Magazine published a report on this activity in July, 1963.

SINCE THEN, enormous strides have been made as the townsfolk came to understand their problems. The electorate approved a levy for a new fire hall and fire equipment last September—a project on which the club had worked four years. Without the groundwork laid by Vesta members in a program of education and of persistence with the city council, the new fire hall never would have come into being.

The women had a head-long fight with city officials, the council members having refused to cooperate with the volunteer firemen as to site, kind of building or willingness to put a measure on the ballot. The women made a mock-up with scale models of the fire equipment to prove to the council that a suggested garage building wasn't large enough. They sent representatives to every council meeting to insure consideration of the fire hall need.

The volunteer firemen would have given up their campaign for a fire hall long ago if the club had not persisted.

When the levy election day came

the Vestas really worked to get out the vote. Mrs. Bowen described the election-day activities in her report to the Federation. It follows, in part:

"Watching the polls we find only 80 have voted by noon. We need 215 to validate the election. We list their names, check our lists and start calling. We offer rides and baby-sitting. By 3 o'clock our calls and the sound car have produced results. Two hundred have voted. Between 6 and 8 o'clock the vote is so heavy we worry. Are they turning out in such numbers to approve the levy or vote it down? Past experience with our school elections doesn't give us confidence.

"At 8:30 comes the news! The fire hall passed by 86 per cent and the fire truck by 92 per cent. The firemen feel as if their community has just given them the medal of honor."

The Bowens (he is fire chief) drove the new fire rig home from New York after the Federation convention.

WHEN the women began their efforts the town was involved in a serious school-site issue and was pulling apart at the seams with innumerable conflicts. Families with school children were moving away because the voters 11 times had turned down bonds for a badly needed new high school to replace the old firetrap, closed by the state fire marshal.

As with the fire levy the women worked hard for passage of the high-school proposal which finally was approved last December.

Mrs. Bowen's report noted that most businessmen and community leaders had made little effort to solve the high-school problem. The school board meetings were sparsely attended and 14 of 32 teachers had resigned. It was to stem the tide of bitterness and dis-

In cab: Mrs. Gerald McKinney; atop truck, Mrs. Dick James; in front, from left: Mrs. Charles Bowen, Mrs. Darrel Sweat, Mrs. Charles Reynolds and Mrs. Warren Delzer.—Photos by Robert Rembold.

Opposite. Winter in
Leavenworth offers
spectacular vistas.
Norwegian Magnus Bakke
designed four ski jumps at
this nearby mountain, and
for many years Bakke Hill
became the site of a national
ski jumping competition.
Today, the lower slopes are
used by downhill skiers,
while cross-country
enthusiasts find miles of
tracks nearby. The annual
Ice Fest sculpture contest
draws artists from miles
around, and ice skating on a
new artificial lake near
downtown promises to be a
popular attraction.

Award, a $10,000 grant in recognition of their community service. Shirley asked if the presentation of the Sears Award could be made at the newly approved Autumn Leaf Festival, to be held a couple of months later. She thought, rightly, that more people would come to the award presentation if it were made a highlight of the festival. I quickly agreed that this was a wonderful idea. To my disbelief, when the final report of our meeting was issued, however, there was scant mention of either the Alpine theme for Leavenworth or the Autumn Leaf Festival. How frustrating this was!

Afterwards, I was looking for other ways to introduce these same ideas when Ken Nyberg, who replaced Dirk Anderson as consultant for Project LIFE, made an excellent suggestion. He said I should join another LIFE team, the Labor and Industries Committee, and continue working on my proposals there. And that is what I did.

Project LIFE did bring cooperation and more trust back into the community. The September 20, 1964 *Seattle Sunday Times* carried this item:

> *The Vestas noted that the project was 'good therapy for our town....We needed to know working together was possible and we needed something of which to be proud.'...Bob Brender (the LIFE chairman) says that the wounds have virtually healed in Leavenworth. He believes that the recreation report, throwing new light on superb recreation facilities and a study of tourism, may solve the economic problems. For the tourism report showed that the town has the ability to provide food, shelter and other accommodations as well as magnificent scenery.*

A Resistance to "Outsiders" and Change

Many of the setbacks Bob and I faced as we tried to gain acceptance for our ideas—both during Project LIFE and later on—stemmed from our status as outsiders. As Pauline Watson once told us:

> *Small town merchants don't want to be told what to do, and they don't want to be told by somebody from out of town. That is the number one thing....You folks had lived in Seattle before...and now you're trying to tell us what we should do. It was going over like a bomb! Not that it wasn't a good idea, it was simply coming from the outside. A city feller trying to tell us people how we should do our business, and we'll ignore him, is what we'll do!*

At first, the only way the townspeople had known us was through The Squirrel Tree and the only comment we heard about was, "Well, they won't

last over six months up there." As Bob and I became more involved in the affairs of Leavenworth, however, we became aware of how the townspeople saw us. Bob and I always had to accept the fact that we were outsiders. We were "furiners" in most people's eyes, and we were still considered outsiders five years after we opened The Squirrel Tree simply because the restaurant was fifteen miles out of town. Yet even after we moved our home into downtown Leavenworth, we remained outsiders. I don't mean to imply that everyone in town was opposed to our ideas. Far from it! There were many who whole-heartedly supported our views and encouraged us. Nevertheless, as outsiders, we couldn't avoid the age-old phenomenon of "them and us."

One problem lay in the fact that we didn't take part in many social activities. The social and cultural life of a small town is usually built around families, school activities, churches, sports, clubs and associations and we didn't seem to fit into any of these groups—not one! We were simply very private people—and still are. Actually, we had no social life to speak of, for all our time and energies went into running the restaurant and motel. Later, when remodeling was under way in Leavenworth, our social life consisted of entertaining many out-of-towners at The Squirrel Tree, people who might be helpful in developing tourism. But for some Leavenworth residents we appeared to be "in it" for money alone.

Leavenworth in the early and mid-1960s was full of eyesores like the old Fitz Building on Front Street. Later, the building was purchased and restored by Joe Jackson and Heinz Ulbricht.

The truth is that no one knew how perilously close to bankruptcy we were. From the beginning we decided to put all profits back into the business, especially into efforts for furthering the Alpine theme. Later, as my conviction grew that tourism was right for Leavenworth, I risked all our financial resources by sinking us into great debt. And then I borrowed still more!

One area of trouble we did not foresee had to do with the underlying attitude toward tourism by the average local citizen. We didn't realize what a wrenching change it would be for the people, even though some businesses such as service stations and restaurants became ardent supporters of this change.

In 1969 a research study on tourism in Leavenworth was made by Lance V. Packer. When we read his report, we better understood the resistance and difficulties we'd encountered many years earlier. Packer's report, which should prove very useful to other towns that want to develop tourism as a viable economy, pointed out that tourism "requires a great degree of involvement in human social relationships, which other economies do not require."

Until now, Leavenworth's economy had been based on the making or growing of things such as lumber and fruit, whereas an economy based on tourism would now be dependent on people. It wouldn't do to have tourists treated as undesirable outsiders or "furiners."

Packer confirmed that tourism is an economy just like any other, although it has its own requirements. And he said, "...without the efforts of the community to improve itself (especially through the help of the LIFE program) tourism in Leavenworth could not have developed, nor can it continue without it."

At that time, though, not even the city council supported those of us willing to take the risk of remodeling. Later when one council member who had been very much against tourism sold his business for a handsome profit, he said, "Well, if it hadn't been for this project, I'd never have got my business sold like I did."

Fortunately, today, with the many changes of character Leavenworth has gone through, the "outsider" no longer experiences what we did thirty-five years ago.

Authenticity—Essential For a "Theme" Town to Succeed

At The Squirrel Tree we learned a great deal about what was required to create and maintain a theme business. In particular, we learned that a theme

"We didn't go into The Squirrel Tree to make money because we both had good jobs. And later when we came up with this idea about remodeling Leavenworth, it may be hard to believe, but again it wasn't the thought of making money. It was just something we really wanted to do. We must have been looking through rose-colored glasses, because nobody, including us, could foresee the success that was generated there in Leavenworth. Nobody could."
—Bob Rodgers

must be carried out in as authentic a manner as possible. Authenticity, for some people in Leavenworth, became quite a controversial subject. What exactly did it mean to be authentic? Why did Bob Rodgers and I make such a large issue of authenticity? And how could such financially depressed building owners afford great additional expenses for the sake of authenticity?

Right from the beginning, the biggest obstacle to establishing authenticity was the cost. We knew we could effect "a Bavarian look" in a superficial way—and at a relatively low cost. For instance, we could have put up scalloping or shakes to imitate a roofline, installed full shutters and window boxes, used lots of paint, added Alpine ornamentation and called it "Bavarian."

But Bob and I decided we had to vigorously oppose anything less than an authentic remodeling. To create a successful Bavarian village we would have to be as thorough and accurate as we could in all details of construction. A high level of craftsmanship was definitely needed.

Pre-Alpine Developments: 1964-65

The transformation of Leavenworth to a Bavarian village—that is, the actual remodeling of the town—began with just six building owners. When we first committed ourselves to the venture, we dubbed the plan "Project Alpine." Prior to this, however, some of the other building owners had improved their storefronts by applying a fresh coat of paint or adding a trim or modern design. These included the Stroup Building, Seattle First National Bank, Chuck Bergman Barber Shop Building, Norris Hardware and Larsen Drug Store.

These were some of the best downtown buildings, and they occupied key locations. As I watched their efforts to spruce up their buildings, I saw in my mind's eye Bavarian storefronts being added and wondered, "Now that they've gone to this expense will they listen to my ideas of an Alpine theme? Can they even afford to listen?"

Even if the townspeople did agree to a theme town I was afraid they might decide on a Gay 90s theme. There was already the Pink Garter Theatre, which in the early 1960s had a delightful and popular Gay Nineties Review featuring a show-stopping performance by "The Rosebuds," some of the hulkiest, hairiest, most masculine-looking men in Leavenworth.

Even Mike Wolfe, a consultant from the Department of Architecture at the University of Washington, urged us to restore the fronts of the buildings

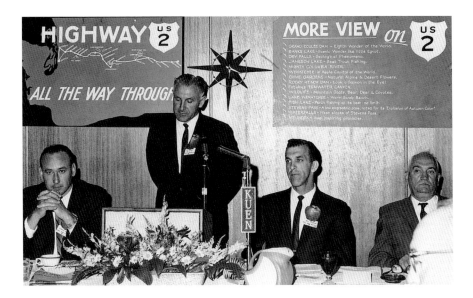

At our first tourist school in Leavenworth, we learned what tourism could do for our economy and what we could give in return. Here, I'm addressing the group as chairman of the Project LIFE Tourism Committee. Seated, left to right, are Hartley Kruger, Division of Tourism, Washington State Department of Commerce and Economic Development; Bob Rodgers, president of the U.S. Highway 2 Association and an unidentified speaker.

to their original condition and adopt a turn-of-the-century, or perhaps a Gay Nineties, theme. Another group strongly supported a Western theme.

I had many ideas for winning approval of the Bavarian theme, and not all of them were successful. By no means! For instance, I thought it would help if people could see my vision illustrated. Our customers at The Squirrel Tree really liked the exterior fireplace mural of the Alpine mountain climber, so in early 1964 I hired the same artist, Baroness Margaret Von Wrangel, to do a painting of the main street downtown (Front Street) as though it were the center of a Bavarian town. Unfortunately, the painting didn't show the buildings completely in a Bavarian design, so it could not be presented.

The First Tourism School

In June 1964 Bob and I arranged for the first major tourism school to be held in Leavenworth. While working with the Washington U.S. Highway 2 Association I had made important contacts at the state capital, Olympia, especially in the Department of Commerce and Economic Development's Division of Tourism. So under the auspices of the Tourist Committee of Project LIFE and the Highway 2 committees, I invited key government officials to Leavenworth to conduct a program on tourism. Then I worked with the state to bring in officials from the American Automobile Association and Northwest Airlines.

The tourism school became an essential program for helping everyone in town and other nearby towns—not just merchants and their employees—to

Danish Solvang in the mid-1960s. Before its transformation, Solvang had been a typical California town with Spanish architecture. Our first visit there convinced us that Leavenworth's architecture could change, too, and become Bavarian in the best sense of the word.

understand all aspects of tourism as an industry and to foster a gradual acceptance of this industry in Leavenworth. Those conducting the school emphasized two primary things visitors take home with them—what they see and memorable feelings about the friendly people they meet.

We were urged to put our best foot forward, to treat visitors with the same consideration and respect we ourselves might want. We were also told that a tourist dollar could turn over fourteen or more times within the greater community. We learned later that the Washington officials in tourism considered ours perhaps the most successful tourism school they'd ever taught.

Solvang, California—A Danish Village

My dreams and unfolding vision of a Bavarian theme town began to become a reality when in early January 1965 Bob and I visited Solvang, California during our annual trip to the Los Angeles Gift Show to buy merchandise for our souvenir shop at The Squirrel Tree. Bob's sister had told us of this small California town, which was a very successful tourist attraction, and in 1965 we decided to find out how the townspeople's experience there might benefit Leavenworth.

Some Danes lived in Solvang, so naturally they influenced the adoption of the Danish architectural theme that transformed their town into a "little Denmark." As a replica of an Old World town, Solvang looked authentic— and it was very successful. We were impressed with what we saw, especially with the charming atmosphere the Danish theme created, and we saw enormous numbers of visitors and a thriving tourist economy.

During our stay, I talked to as many people as I could about such matters as how they got started, how much things cost, where their financing came from. We met the man who conceived the idea originally and initiated the transformation. And I took photographs and brought back postcards to show Leavenworth residents how such a project could work for us, too.

One day we dropped into a bakery, where Bob Rodgers overheard two waitresses talking. One said, "Boy, we sure had a slow day. We just took in a little over $600." Well, to us at that time, $600 was an astronomical amount. There probably weren't many stores in Leavenworth that took in even $100 a day! So when Bob told that story to the people back home, they didn't believe him. They thought he was making it up—$600 was simply too much!

After we saw Solvang, we knew for certain we were on the right track—if only we could find a way to finance the remodeling that would be required in Leavenworth. People were strapped financially and many might not be able to get loans, although they would have to borrow the entire cost of remodeling their buildings.

Once again we were plunging into an endeavor for which we had no experience, other than developing the theme at The Squirrel Tree. There were going to be hundreds of problems—fortunately, more than we could possibly anticipate at that time. Yet I knew it wasn't just a dream. I knew in my heart it could work and somehow now was the time, in spite of how destitute most people were.

I determined to give it literally everything I had—physically, mentally, and financially—and as events were to show I gave it so much I nearly went over the edge in all three departments!

When we returned from California, I immediately began telling anyone who would listen about Solvang. I was still serving on the Labor and Industry Committee of Project LIFE and was more eager than ever to talk about tourism and a Bavarian theme. Some people got pretty tired of hearing me, too! I wrote a ten-page report on tourism for the committee in which I mentioned Solvang and included a proposal for off-street parking.

The report was not well received by some on the committee. Instead, many wanted to condemn certain riverfront properties and offer sites to one

". . . the Autumn Festival President, Shirley Bowen, had made the remark to us that Ted Price was the Vice-President of the Autumn Festival, and all he kept talking about was some crazy town called Solvang. And she was very upset, because she could care less about what happened in Solvang!"
— Pauline Watson

"The Tumwater Politicians" were yours truly (top), Bob Brender (bottom) and Vern Herrett, owner of the Tumwater Cafe. Unfortunately, I was unable to acquire a photo of Vern.

or more manufacturing industries—a furniture manufacturer, a brewery, a vodka plant or other bottling works, fruit-processing and juice industries—in fact, any manufacturing industry that might provide jobs.

This was a terrible blow. My motives and general plans seemed to be misunderstood and sometimes mistrusted. I was told the chairperson of the committee remarked more than once, "Solvang, Solvang, Solvang! If Ted Price likes it so much, why doesn't he move there!" Now, once again, when the final report of the Labor and Industry Committee was released, it was disheartening to discover that my tourism report was not included—even though I had barely mentioned Solvang!

"The Tumwater Politicians"

During this time, the burden of running our restaurant and motel was falling largely on Bob's shoulders. My time and energy were more and more expended in different committee meetings, as well as in informal talks with various people in town. Those were days of meetings, meetings, meetings!

Of particular importance and enjoyment were the early morning coffee sessions with Bob Brender and Vern Herrett. Almost every morning Bob and I were the first customers at the Tumwater Cafe, which Vern owned. This is how Bob Brender describes those meetings:

> *The purpose was to come up with new ideas and thinking on how to improve our community here. We'd have a cup of coffee and if other citizens would happen to drop in the coffee shop, we'd invite them to sit down with us....Yet it got back to us one day that we were called "the Tumwater politicians." Now we weren't doing any politics at all. We were just trying to better our community.*

To this day Bob Brender and Vern Herrett have not received full recognition for their major contributions to Leavenworth's development.

Vern and Ann Herrett were much respected members of the community. Vern was a leader in the Democratic party, who—along with county officials—was later instrumental in developing the parks and acquiring Blackbird Island for park use. Vern moved very quietly, without fanfare, except when he ran for mayor.

For his part, Bob Brender liked the idea of having a Bavarian motif for the buildings in downtown Leavenworth and was extremely supportive of all efforts to bring in tourism. When he discovered that not everyone in the LIFE committees shared his enthusiasm, he looked for ways to further tourism within the chamber of commerce, of which he was then president. Early in 1965, as a gesture of solid support, he appointed me chairman of the Leavenworth Chamber of Commerce Tourism Committee and asked me to help invite outside speakers on tourism. This charge enabled me to contact the people I'd already met—from the state government, the media and other professional fields—who could help us.

For Sale—The Squirrel Tree

For Bob and me Solvang had been an inspiration, but now it was time for us to act. So we put The Squirrel Tree up for sale and set about looking for property. We were prepared to take the lead, drawing upon our experience at The Squirrel Tree as well as what we learned about Solvang, and we trusted that the time would come when we could raise enough money to engage an architect. As we searched, we found property prices to be extremely low. In fact, many building owners had difficulty selling at any price.

The downtown buildings and other properties we bought were:

Hobo Gulch, 24+ acres, with about a half-mile of river frontage (now Bayern Village) $12,000

Brown House, 8th Street, river view $2,000

Farrimond Building, 8th Street $2,500

McKenzie Barber Shop Building, 8th Street $1,000

King property, 4 houses; 11 lots $4,100

Coontz Building (now the Tannenbaum) $9,000

Reeve's Bakery Building, Front Street $10,750

Most of these properties were vacant or unwanted buildings. Had they been located elsewhere in Washington, however, they would have cost much more. We purchased most buildings through Ted Adams, Leavenworth's local realtor who had his Front Street realty office and his apartment in our Coontz (Tannenbaum) Building. At this time we sank everything we had and everything we could borrow into real estate. We really stuck our necks out to the point of courting bankruptcy, because our restaurant and motel hadn't yet sold. To some, our commitment to buying property proved our total confidence in remodeling the town, but to others it seemed that "Price and Rodgers practically own the town!"

Ted Adams was our only apartment renter. He paid $20 a month and, for his Front Street office, $35 a month, while we paid for water, sewer and

LaVerne Peterson owned two large buildings on Front Street. From the very beginning her unquestioned faith in adopting a Bavarian theme led her to risk everything and plunge into debt to remodel her Chikamin Hotel as the Edelweiss.

garbage amounting to nearly one-fourth of those amounts. When we tried to raise Ted's rents by $10 and $15 respectively, however, he moved out and found cheaper space.

The other residences we owned were low-income houses, located near downtown, and they were seldom rented. Still, there were problems. Some tenants made many demands, while others did no maintenance—not even removing heavy snow from their roofs and porches—and still others wouldn't even pay their rent. We really did not want to be landlords, but for a time we were trapped.

For both Bob and me, pressure was building steadily. Each day I drove back and forth into Leavenworth to attend meetings, while trying to handle my responsibilities at The Squirrel Tree. I often fell behind, and this created excessive demands on Bob.

A Breakthrough!

A breakthrough for introducing the Bavarian architectural style occurred in the spring of 1965, thanks to Pauline Watson, LaVerne Vincent Peterson and Vern Herrett—three longtime residents of Leavenworth who were completely dedicated to helping their town. (LaVerne later remarried, so I will use her present name, LaVerne Peterson.)

LaVerne had purchased the old Chikamin Hotel on the corner of Front Street and Ninth following a disastrous fire in 1962 that destroyed the second-floor rooms. She had borrowed a large sum of money to rebuild the interior of the hotel, but she had not planned to remodel the exterior until it was discovered that many of the window sills had to be replaced.

The Chikamin Hotel occupied a prominent corner downtown and would be an ideal "first" building to adopt the Bavarian architectural style. As soon as Bob and I heard LaVerne might remodel the exterior, we hoped to persuade her to "go Bavarian," but how, since we didn't know her well? Then one day at The Squirrel Tree I received a phone call from Pauline Watson, saying that LaVerne needed to make some repairs on the outside of her building and was open to suggestions as to style or design. Pauline and her husband Owen owned and operated an electric shop downtown. We didn't know each other well, but Pauline had certainly heard through the grapevine about "Ted Price and that damned Solvang!" So Pauline suggested I bring my slides of Solvang to show her, Owen and LaVerne and a few others who were interested.

Needless to say, I leapt at the opportunity. That evening Bob and I went to the back room of the Watsons' store, where we showed the slides and told our story. Pauline said that if we could convince LaVerne, the other building owners would be much more likely to come along.

She was right. LaVerne was very impressed. After she'd seen the slides and listened to our ideas, she simply stood up and said, "I've got to get back to work, but that's good enough for me. Count me in!"

I believe that was the moment when the Bavarian theme actually took hold. Pauline and Owen Watson were also ready to remodel their building, and that night all of us agreed to make every effort to see the Chikamin Hotel become the first Bavarian-style building in town. Bob said of Pauline, "One of her biggest contributions to getting the town done was that she'd lived there all her life, the people were familiar with her, and she could probably convince people a lot easier than we could that this was the right thing to do."

LaVerne was already in debt from remodeling the fire-damaged rooms in her hotel, and she couldn't really afford more large-scale remodeling. Nevertheless, gutsy and quietly determined as she was, she negotiated a large additional loan and began looking for Bavarian-style designs. Soon she renamed

Front Street in 1965 showing three of the first six buildings before remodeling: (from left) LaVerne Peterson's Chikamin Hotel and Vern and Ann Herrett's Cascade Drug Store and PUD Building. Seated (right) is Pauline Watson, whose infectious enthusiasm for the project led her to sketch some of the downtown buildings, applying Bavarian designs. Bob Rodgers and Oleg Warnek also prepared sketches before we adopted Earl Petersen's approach—an insistence on complete authenticity, particularly in roof construction.

the Chikamin the Hotel Edelweiss, after the name of the state flower of Bavaria.

Bob and I, too, were ready to borrow money to begin remodeling at least one of the buildings we were buying—that is, if we could still borrow money. Then one morning over coffee at the Tumwater Cafe, I spoke to Vern Herrett about how vital it was that the buildings on Front Street be remodeled first. Vern was much respected in town and owned two buildings adjoining LaVerne's Chikamin Hotel—the Cascade Drug Store Building and the PUD Building (currently der Sportsman and the Hotel Europa). Vern smiled and said, "I don't know why I'm agreeing to do this. Here I am, eighty years old, with one foot in the grave and the other foot on a banana peel. And here I am agreeing to do this!" In remodeling these two buildings right at the beginning, Vern and his wife Ann had to postpone remodeling their Tumwater Cafe, which was not on Front Street.

From that point on, I am afraid I left even more work to Bob at The Squirrel Tree, as I drove back and forth to Leavenworth several times a day. Now that the vision was becoming a reality, I talked to everyone in town I could—not only about remodeling, but about many other things that would have to be thought about and accomplished if tourism were indeed to become an industry for Leavenworth.

Meanwhile, Pauline Watson enthusiastically created sketches of some of the storefronts downtown that showed how the existing facades could be made to look Bavarian—at a cost, she thought, of about $500 per building. Soon Oleg Warnek also began making sketches, as did Bob Rodgers. Later, Pauline said, "If anybody had told us what [the costs] would be, you wouldn't see Building One here yet, I don't believe. We would have all fainted away! And that would have been the end of it....We started out thinking in terms of maybe $500 we'd spend. And you know, after the first $500 had gone through your mind, it's a little easier to add another $200 or $300 to that."

~ 5 ~

Leavenworth Goes Alpine!

"We had lived here all our lives and probably would be like the others that didn't really want our village to change, but we wanted it to stay here and be alive. I can understand the people that objected to the changing of their hometown. You know, the 'I don't want to change [attitude],' without realizing that if it didn't change, it wouldn't be here! It was going to die, and we would be a ghost town! And so it had to change."

— *Pauline Watson*

"A small town which through sheer guts pulled itself up by its bootstraps."
— *A visitor from Santa Barbara*

On Thursday evening, June 10, 1965, about twenty people came to the Tumwater Cafe to hear presentations from Pauline Watson and Bob Rodgers. They included Wilbur Bon, mayor; Bob Brender, chamber president; Russell and Vera Lee, publishers of *The Echo* and several of us building owners.

Pauline showed sketches of some Leavenworth buildings remodeled in a Bavarian design, and we displayed pictures of Solvang and posters of Old German towns. Bob told the gathering, "This is no small thing. I don't know if any of us realizes the economic as well as aesthetic impact it will have on this community." But Pauline summed up our message, saying, "There are some of us who are ready to remodel our stores. We would like to do them with an Alpine theme, such as shown here tonight. We are asking for an agreement from each of you that if and when you re-do your building, you will follow this theme."

THE LEAVENWORTH ECHO

SERVING THE UPPER WENATCHEE VALLEY --- THE RECREATIONAL CENTER OF THE STATE

VOLUME 64   LEAVENWORTH, CHELAN COUNTY, WASHINGTON   NUMBER 24   10c a Copy   THURSDAY, JUNE 17, 1965

Leavenworth Goes "Alpine"

Bavarian Alpine Store Fronts Are Favored

Leavenworth merchants are going to do what comes naturally. Midst natural Alpine surroundings they are going to adopt Bavarian Alpine architecture for store fronts.

This was the decision made by about 20 merchants at a meeting last Thursday night. Already the announcement has brought enthusiastic approval from people here and outside of the area.

Half a dozen owners of store buildings have expressed their intention to go ahead with the design. Pauline Watson has drawn designs for the Chikamin Hotel and S&I Tavern, both drug store buildings, the Hornet apartment building, the Icicle Tavern building, Watson Electric and the building occupied by Scenic Market.

Bavarian Alpine design includes the use of much of the present brick construction with the addition of some stucco. Numerous window shutters, window boxes and scalloped designs in wood add to the Bavarian touch. European "half-timbering" is used and designs are routed into the wood or painted on it. Additions of window shutters in the second windows, a window box at the bottom portion of the building, direct lighting under a shaked over the map would transform ugly scene on Front street to attractive spot.

The merchants appointed a committee Thursday night to coordinate the details of the movement. It will also be presented at next Chamber of Commerce meeting. Chairman of the committee Pauline Watson and assistant Bob Rodgers. Other members for include Evelyn Larson, Lorne Vincent and Betty McKerlie.

Pauline Watson, who has already devoted many hours on the drawing, presented the idea to merchants, stating that it is more than just another beautification project. It is a program to make Leavenworth the destination for tourists, to create business. It is also designed to attract the family type of visitor, not the "carnival" type.

Bob Rodgers commented on enthusiasm voiced by outside

Every person there consented. It was simply a gentlemen's agreement, but it proved to be as binding as a signed document. Before the meeting ended, several building owners committed to "go Alpine."

We named our venture Project Alpine, which became a new committee of the Leavenworth Chamber of Commerce. Pauline served as chairperson, with Bob Rodgers as vice-chair, until the beginning of 1966, when she and Bob served as co-chairs. The duty of this committee was to initiate, coordinate and guide the remodeling, as well as all other activities and events related to the Bavarian transformation. Construction was to conceal modern-day conveniences, such as antennas, to create a village that might have been found a century or two ago in Old Bavaria.

Everyone had agreed LaVerne's Edelweiss Hotel should be the first building to be remodeled. The Edelweiss, as a Bavarian hotel in a key location, would be an ideal tourist attraction, one easily seen from Highway 2. We knew that the first building to be remodeled would receive wide publicity, and LaVerne was ready to move ahead even though she'd have to borrow thousands of dollars more than she'd originally planned. In the next edition of *The Leavenworth Echo*, June 17, 1965, our historic meeting and its outcome were announced in a large headline: "Leavenworth Goes Alpine!"

With Project Alpine launched, we needed widescale publicity. A key person in attaining it was Hank Pearson in the Tourism Division of the Washington State Department of Commerce and Economic Development. Hank's office in Olympia created press releases and other forms of publicity and sent them to regional newspapers and other media. After I phoned Hank to introduce Pauline as the chairperson of our new Alpine Committee, press releases from Olympia on Leavenworth's revitalization carried Pauline's name as the primary contact. This is one of the ways Pauline gradually became spokesperson for many of the developments in Leavenworth.

Even though the momentum for going Alpine had increased considerably by this time, some people still resented my presence in a leadership role. Was this due to an underlying fear of change, to my being an outsider, or to jealousy? In my own mind, I had already decided to work behind the scenes as much as possible. Later, Vera Lee told me, "I think if you had taken the credit and stepped out in the limelight with this thing, it'd never gone....It wouldn't have worked if you'd have stayed in front of it all the time."

In those days there was another project that also needed to be done—drawing up Leavenworth's first parks and recreation plan. Besides, there were things to be accomplished outside Leavenworth—contacting people I knew for immediate publicity and finding more new people who might prove helpful. I knew that word of Leavenworth's "Going Alpine" would soon reach our Project LIFE consultants in Seattle, so I contacted Mike Wolfe in the Department of Architecture at the University of Washington. When I told him of our decision to go Bavarian, I had to move the receiver away from my ear. My best recollection of what Mike said was this: "You can't do that—you're not a German town. It would be dishonest to take a German theme. You'd end up being a cuckoo clock town!"

Mike was the expert and people listened to him. Consequently, I was worried that the whole project might collapse, so I said, "Mike, if you say something like that now to the people here, it'll split us, and then nothing will get done." Mike replied, "If they ask me, I'll have to tell them." But he agreed to think about it and to send me a letter. Fortunately, no one ever officially asked Mike's opinion.

Before the first construction and remodeling got under way, we were only a handful of people who were broke and promoting very big, seemingly impractical ideas. We knew we were taking a major risk, and that meant sacrifices. Yet a certain pride kept us from seeking financial aid elsewhere, especially from the state or federal government.

The city council provided no support either. Many of us believed that council members simply thought we were unrealistic and harmless. Ironically, their lack of interest enabled us to move more quickly, freely and creatively! LaVerne said in an interview, "I know that talking to a couple of the (city) council members, ... Whew! they really thought we were just clear out of it. I mean, they had no interest in what we were doing whatsoever!"

At that time, Leavenworth was so poor it could not afford a city manager or city planner. The volunteer Leavenworth Planning Commission didn't seem interested. They were totally inexperienced in such matters as remodeling and were so silent the town might as well not have had a planning commission. So we undertook all the planning for Project Alpine ourselves.

Help Appears—From Solvang!

Now that we knew what we wanted to do, how in the world were we to proceed? Where were we going to find the professional architects with experience in the special design techniques required? Bob and I felt it important there be more than one architect—to insure that all the buildings wouldn't have the same facade and the same roof design. But when we found such architects, how could we afford them? This dilemma was resolved in such an easy, natural way that the solution seemed heaven sent.

Ten days after Russ Lee ran *The Leavenworth Echo* headline, "Leavenworth Goes Alpine!" he phoned me at The Squirrel Tree and said, "Ted, you'll never guess who's here...the man who designed about eighty percent of Solvang to Danish—and he has a lot of his designs with him!"

I couldn't believe it. One of the people who could most help us had come on his own to our doorstep! This man was Earl Petersen, to whom Leavenworth owes much, not only for his design work and suggestions but for his firm insistence that we make our building designs and decor authentic in every way.

Because of his success in Solvang, Earl Petersen was looking for another town that was interested in adopting an architectural theme. He had visited Leavenworth about a year before, speculated that the town held potential as a theme town, then subscribed to *The Echo* to keep abreast of the town's affairs. When he saw the headline about Leavenworth going Alpine, he came straight

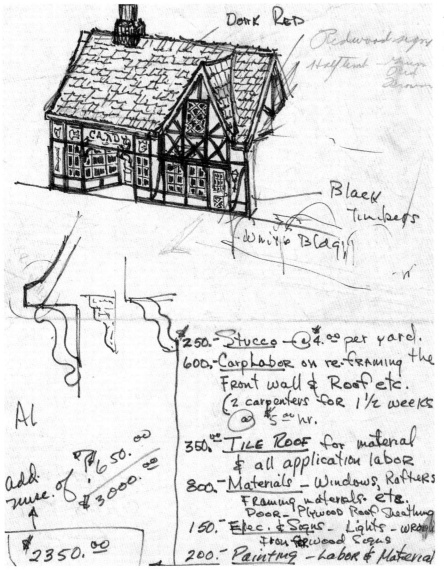

The handwritten notes on the sketch include:

DARK RED

Redwood sign
Halftimb —

Black Timbers

white Bldg

CANDY

Al
add. nue. of $650.00
$3000.00

$2350.00

$250.— Stucco @ $4.00 per yard.
600.— Carp Labor on re-framing the
    Front wall & Roof etc.
    (2 carpenters for 1½ weeks
    @ $5.00 hr.
350.00 Tile Roof for material
    & all application labor
800.— Materials — Windows, Rafters
    Framing materials. etc.
    Door — Plywood Roof Sheathing
150.— Elec. & Signs — Lights — Wrought
    Iron & wood Signs
200.— Painting — Labor & Material

An early sketch of our Bakery Building made by Solvang designer Earl Petersen at an inspiring all-night meeting at The Squirrel Tree in June 1965. Earl also jotted down cost estimates for materials and construction.

away. Earl's interest was far more than casual—he wanted to buy *The Echo* and move to Leavenworth, and he wanted to make some modest investments in real estate.

When Russ phoned that afternoon, I invited him to bring Earl to The Squirrel Tree for dinner. Russ and Vera were very busy printing that week's edition, but they agreed to come that evening, too. I also invited Pauline and Owen Watson and suggested that Pauline bring the sketches she'd made of the existing buildings.

We were all excited, and what a night that was! At dinner we asked Earl many questions and listened with eagerness and anticipation to everything he said. As it grew late, the Watsons and Lees went home but Earl stayed on, explaining design and construction details we simply had known nothing about.

Then, as Bob Rodgers tells it, "We had been sitting there talking and talking and talking, and when I looked out the window, I thought there was a forest fire! I told everybody, 'Look out the window. There's a forest fire out there—on top of the ridge across from The Squirrel Tree!' Come to find out, it was just the sun coming up—we had talked all night long!"

That night was truly an inspiration, and it was another turning point. Earl had added a ringing endorsement to our insistence that everything about our Bavarian buildings appear to be authentic, saying, "If you can't do it right, don't do anything! Or wait until you can do it right!"

Of all the major elements of design and construction Earl discussed, he emphasized roofs. If we accomplished nothing else, he said, we must make the roofs appear functional. They should cover the existing building far enough back so that from the street they'd give the impression of covering the whole building. He also stressed that unusable upper stories or lofts should appear to be occupied, which meant installing interior lights and colored window panes to block visibility from the outside.

He explained what would and wouldn't work in stucco, how to achieve numerous authentic details on the buildings and how to achieve the greatest visual impact by keeping them at eye level. In Bavaria centuries ago no one knew how to make large plate glass windows, so their windows were comprised of many small panes. Earl showed us how to simulate this effect by using a hinged framework that fits over plate glass. He also talked about woodworking techniques, urging us to use Old European-style carved wood signs, emphasizing that all business signs should be small and advising us where to buy Old European-style lighting fixtures.

That night Earl quickly sketched out a design for our Bakery Building and quoted a low estimate for the remodeling. He further surprised us by announcing that he'd give designs to all those who wanted to remodel. Although he was extremely busy in Solvang, he offered to design Leavenworth buildings free of charge! The Chikamin/Edelweiss was the first project we presented to him.

Earl Petersen's sudden, miraculous appearance in Leavenworth ushered in Project Alpine with a bang. Given the number of buildings he had designed in Solvang, Earl possessed considerable experience and building skill in relation to Old Europe. The incredible thing was that he was not even a registered architect—but he was a terrific designer!

Influential People Speak on Authenticity

Earl's insistence on authenticity helped set the stage for the Chamber of Commerce meeting a few nights later. Construction was going to begin soon, and it was important that the highest standards be set in the first buildings remodeled. In this regard, I'd invited three influential speakers to address the meeting.

An excellent talk that night was given by Marjorie Phillips of the Washington State Arts Commission. Bob and I met Marjorie in about 1963 when the scenic highway sign laws were being enacted. Another speaker, Betty Evans, a writer for *The Seattle Times*, had already given Leavenworth excellent coverage for Project LIFE. The third speaker was Al Goldblatt, Betty's husband and a marketing expert.

I believe it was Al who said that night, "If you're going to put up something that's going to blow down in a month or a year, forget it, because tourists can see through it." I had asked each speaker to emphasize one point

A Washington State Arts Commission dinner meeting at the Tumwater Cafe in 1965. This was an unusual event for Leavenworth. Left photo. Margaret Motteler, Royal Lady of the 1965 Washington State Autumn Leaf Festival; Bob Brender, president of the Leavenworth Chamber of Commerce and other dignitaries. Right photo. Marjorie Phillips of the Washington State Arts Commission is seated second from right, next to Huntington Boyd, now a prominent Leavenworth businessman. Ken Brooks (seated at far end of table) presides.

only—make it authentic, or don't do it at all. They told us not even to think about remodeling unless we were prepared to do a comprehensive, first-class job of creating a Bavarian village. They said we must get the best professional help available.

After that meeting, the enthusiasm for creating an authentic-looking village was very strong. Everybody seemed to be for it! The meeting also convinced us that somehow we had to engage several professional designers in order to achieve some variety in our building designs.

Now, I thought, was the time for the townspeople to start calling Leavenworth a Bavarian village, for in doing so we could begin establishing the right atmosphere—for change and for a new life. One morning over coffee I was discussing this idea with Bob Brender, the chamber president. He listened awhile, then frowned and reminded me that officially Leavenworth was classified as a third-class city! The town had gone backwards enough, and Bob didn't like the idea of creating the image of a little village. Before long, though, he supported the idea wholeheartedly because he too wanted tourism for Leavenworth.

The question of what to call the town took other forms as well. Many times over the years some people have wanted to change its name. "Leavenworth," they argued, did not sound Bavarian enough and would remind prospective visitors of the federal prison in Kansas. Once, at a chamber meeting, Bob Brender had heard enough of this and announced that the name "Leavenworth" was not to be changed! There was much applause from those attending. Jokingly, Bob then suggested that a name change might be made for two hills on the edge of town—Big Rattlesnake and Little Rattlesnake.

Heinz Ulbricht

Within one month of Earl Petersen's appearance, another designer—Heinz Ulbricht—simply walked into town and announced he was ready to work for us! Heinz became the designer for most of the remodeled buildings in town. He had read about Leavenworth's decision to adopt a Bavarian theme in *The Seattle Times*, promptly phoned our chamber of commerce, asked how to contact our Alpine Committee and was put in touch with our chairperson, Pauline Watson.

Heinz had already done some Old European-style work in the Northwest. He'd designed and built the Old English Inn in Victoria, British Co-

lumbia, and created a special Old World design near Seattle at a Federal Way shopping mall. I believe he was more knowledgeable about the details of Old Bavarian construction than anyone I have ever known. To our amazement, he offered to design buildings without even a down payment. Then, only if the owner liked the design and used it would he charge for it—and the fee would be very modest. We could hardly believe it!

Moreover, Heinz was ready to start work immediately. For several months, while his family remained in Seattle, he commuted regularly, some 120 miles. Later, his wife Christa, daughter Barbara and son Mike all moved to Leavenworth.

Both Heinz Ulbricht and Earl Petersen proved that genuine talent for design and an insistence on excellence, as well as a broad knowledge of the Bavarian style, were far more important for Leavenworth than accreditation as architects. Thus, the stage was set for the actual work of transforming a decrepit and ailing Leavenworth into the wondrous Bavarian village that exists today.

"Heinz was a real gift to us. I felt that fate sent him to us at just the right moment, because without him, we would never have had the village that we've got now."
— Pauline Watson

"Heinz Ulbricht, I know on his design, his work, he only got paid half of what he wanted because he knew that it was all borrowed money. And I just told him, I said: 'Heinz, I don't have very much money.' And so that's what he settled for. I know he did a lot of work and didn't get paid the price that he should have gotten...."
— LaVerne Peterson

From the 1966 Sunshine Edition of The Leavenworth Echo (front page)

LEAVENWORTH FACE LIFTING -- The Leavenworth business district is getting its face lifted as several business houses assume the "Alpine Look." In process of conversion to Bavarian style are (above) left to right, the Haus Shen Bakery and Tannen Baum Square, at far right. Both buildings are owned by Ted Price and Bob Rodgers, operators of the Squirel Tree Restraunt and leaders in the project. At left center is the first completely coverted Alpine front, housing the Alpin Haus Gift Shoppe and Watson Electric Co.

The First Six Buildings
Lead The Way
1965-66

*"The remarkable thing was that each new storefront was financed
individually and without federal assistance ...and this for a town
economically depressed to the point it barely had two nickels to rub
together."*

— *Ken Nyberg, University of Washington*

By the fall of 1965 planning for remodeling the first six buildings was
under way, and the owners were busy talking to designers and contractors, arranging for financing, and obtaining city building permits. We wanted
to move as fast as possible because the first snow would likely be coming in a
couple of months. Of necessity, we moved forward somewhat independently,
although we kept one another informed of our individual plans.

Because Earl Petersen had offered his services free of charge, four of us—
LaVerne Petserson, Vern Herrett, Bob Rodgers and I—chipped in $150 for
Earl's plane fare from Solvang. This enabled him to return to Leavenworth
and concentrate on a design for the first building, the Edelweiss Hotel. Within
a few weeks after his return to Solvang, Earl submitted the finished drawings
but they still had to be approved by the city council.

Imagine our disappointment when the council rejected his design! The
reason was sound, however. Earl had made the hotel roof long and steep and
the council believed it would pose safety problems. Leavenworth often has
snow from December to April, which sometimes piles up to depths of five to
six feet. Occasionally, thick ice builds up under the snow, forming large icicles
that drop on the sidewalk below. On a long steep roof, ice and snow can also

Top. Earl Petersen's initial design for LaVerne Peterson's Edelweiss Hotel. The design could not be used because the long, steep roof might pose safety problems when snowfalls were heavy.
Above. Heinz Ulbricht's design was the one finally adopted.
Below. The Watson Building (center) was the first to be remodeled, in the fall of 1965.

slide, causing an avalanche to fall on pedestrians. Later, most of us adopted the traditional Bavarian-style roof which has a gentle slope and—often—snow guards on the lower edge.

The council's decision was a blow because it left LaVerne at Square One, and by now Earl couldn't leave Solvang to work on a new plan. If LaVerne had to wait until early the following year to begin remodeling, we wondered, would our little group lose its momentum and enthusiasm? Fortunately, we didn't have to wait because the Watsons were able to move ahead right away. Owen Watson tells the story:

> *Heinz Ulbricht, who designed most of the buildings that are in town now, came over to talk to us. We took him out to dinner, and he saw the print-sketch we had of what we were going to do to the building. And he says, 'Well, let me see if I can come up with something different....I'll go home and you'll have it Tuesday.' And we said we'd have to have it soon because Monday the carpenter was going to be there to start tearing the front of the building down, to get down to the main roof line. And true, Tuesday morning we had the sketch of the building. And that's the way our building was built. We had no blueprints of any kind, so that was something new for the building contractor, too. Because he had nothing to go by, except just a picture of what it was supposed to look like when it was finished.*

LaVerne's Edelweiss Hotel, being remodeled in early spring, 1966.

On September 14, 1965, the scaffolding went up on the Watsons' building and construction began. Today this building is the Alpen Haus.

The other five buildings required designs that were more complex. By the time their architectural plans were completed and approved, the winter would be upon us. Heinz created three more designs: LaVerne's new Edelweiss Hotel and Vern and Ann Herrett's Cascade Drug Store and PUD buildings. LaVerne recalls,

So Ted Price and I went to Seattle and met with Heinz Ulbricht, and he drew a design of my place and sent it back to me....Mr. Herrett and I sat out on the back steps, and we finally decided we would go ahead and try and do the design. We went together, like the things that went on the roof,... and everything would be cheaper for us to go together on it.

Heinz proved to have an unerring sense of what was right for Leavenworth. He knew structural limitations and was knowledgeable about Old European architectural styles and decorative motifs. He was an earnest, hard worker, and as the Bavarianization of the town proceeded, he took on contracting jobs himself.

Heinz also had an understanding heart. He, too, had gone through periods of financial adversity, so he knew the hardships some building owners endured for so long. His design fees were low—sometimes too low, to be honest—and his terms of payment were very reasonable. Heinz deserves the

highest praise for making it possible for the building owners to move ahead with construction as quickly as they did.

Meanwhile, Bob and I returned to Solvang and worked closely with Earl Petersen on the designs for our Tannenbaum and Bakery buildings. His designs were ready in December 1965 and soon were approved by Don Avery, an architect in Olympia who had provided the plans for our Squirrel Tree Chalet Motel. Furthermore, Don drew up detailed structural and building plans to insure that the buildings were suitable for snow country.

Our return trip to Solvang proved to be a godsend. For one thing, Earl introduced us to Ferdinand (Ferd) Sorensen, a Dane and a specialist in techniques for quickly aging and antiquing wood. Ferd promised to help us assure an authentic job on our buildings, so we provided him with transportation to Leavenworth and with housing once he arrived. In return, he agreed to teach local contractors and carpenters special Old European woodworking techniques. The following year, Ferd told us, "You people are so far ahead of us [in Solvang] at this stage that there's no comparison." Ferd was especially helpful to Bob Johnson, Lloyd DeTillian, Bill Guy and others who did the construction.

Top. During the remodeling of our Tannenbaum Building, Ferd Sorensen (center) demonstrates Old World woodworking techniques to Bill Guy (left) and Bob Johnson. Bottom. As construction proceeds on our Bakery Building, Ferd Sorensen (left) double checks architectural details with contractor Lloyd DeTillian (right) and Bill Guy.

Earl also introduced us to Clyde Knight, who moved to Leavenworth for the summer with his wife Ellen. Clyde was a specialist in Old World stucco techniques. In Bavaria, trees were once split by hand, producing rough and irregular timbers. Clyde showed us how to create this same effect on buildings by using stucco and then painting it.

In January 1966 Bob Rodgers became co-chairperson, with Pauline Watson, of Project Alpine. This move strengthened the leadership of the committee. It was fitting, too, that Bob become co-chair, because the Swiss/Bavarian style had originally been Bob's idea when we first remodeled The Squirrel Tree in 1960. Equally important, Bob was always very good with people, as well as being a gifted administrator and a creative problem-solver.

Meanwhile, LaVerne and the Herretts decided to use the same contractor as Bob and I were using to remodel our Tannenbaum Building—Mr. Beve Spears of Cashmere, Washington. The contractor for our Bakery Building was Lloyd "Tweet" DeTillian.

Once her hotel was completed, LaVerne also decided to open the Edelweiss Restaurant, which served the first authentic Bavarian food in Leavenworth. LaVerne had admired Portland, Oregon's famous Rheinlander German Restaurant, so she obtained their menu for guidance. LaVerne's special touch and excellent taste in refurbishing the Edelweiss were most encouraging to the rest of us. But, oh, how tough those early days were. As LaVerne recalls,

> When we opened the Edelweiss, we didn't have any idea what we were going to do. We didn't have all of our furniture yet, and the drapes weren't up. But we opened up, and every day just got a little better and a little better. I remember the first day we took in $500, we were so happy we went home and sat on the floor and counted the money!
>
> When we were starting, I was so far in debt, I mean, I had to work. If I was going to make it at all, I was going to have to just keep on working. But I enjoyed the work. I like waiting on people, and it wasn't that awful hard.

Yet looking back at those important months when the first six buildings were transformed, I don't remember a single time when anyone anticipated anything less than success. Our Project Alpine Committee was a loosely knit group, when you consider its importance in transforming the town. We really had no legal authority, but we did have a strong and single-minded determination to help one another. This spirit of cooperation helped us overcome

THE FIRST SIX BUILDINGS

Building Owner	Name of Building
LaVerne Peterson	Chikamin Hotel (*now Edelweiss Hotel*)
Vern & Ann Herrett	Cascade Drug Store Building (*now Der Sportsman*)
	PUD Building (*now Hotel Europa*)
Pauline & Owen Watson	Watson Electric Building (*now Alpen Haus*)
Ted Price & Bob Rodgers	Bakery Building
	Tannenbaum Building

The Alpen Haus
Opposite page top, left to right. Heinz Ulbricht's original sketch for the Watson Electric Building and a photograph of the building before remodeling began in 1965. A visiting political group from Costa Rica poses in front of the building during reconstruction. This page, top. The Alpen Haus (Watson Building) as it looks today.

Opposite page below and this page below. LaVerne Peterson's Edelweiss Hotel (left) and Vern and Ann Herrett's two adjoining buildings, which today are Der Sportsman and the Europa Hotel.

Transformation of our Bakery Building, the second downtown structure to be remodeled. This page, top. The Bakery Building (right) in 1965. Bob Rodger's early sketch (above). After reconstruction in 1966 (left), following Earl Petersen's design. Below and opposite. Details that made a difference: half-timbering with stucco, flowers in the window box and hanging baskets, carved corbels, a typical Bavarian balcony rail, and European signs that depict the wares available inside the shops.

The Coontz Building becomes the Tannenbaum.
This page, top. The building as it appeared in 1965. Center, left to right: during remodeling in the spring of 1966, a large overhanging roof was added and the front entrance was relocated. Our Tannenbaum Gift Shop (left) specialized in items imported from Europe.

Opposite. Special features of the Tannenbaum included murals by Al Wierich, wood-carved plaques, signs and Bavarian benches by Cliff Hedeen and a glockenspiel in the gable (the title page of this book shows the wooden dancing figures of the glockenspiel that appear every hour on the hour).

73

Artist Kit Clark (left) created detailed models of the first six buildings and two other buildings then under construction. Kit's models were exhibited in other towns to promote Bavarian Leavenworth and its festivals. He also carved the figures for the glockenspiel in our Tannenbaum Building (pictured on the title page).

many difficulties, including personality clashes as our work went forward.

After a mild winter the snow disappeared quickly. Now Leavenworth had its first Bavarian building, and five more would soon appear. You could sense a new awakening for the town—you could feel it everywhere! As very early spring 1966 arrived, construction was under way on five more buildings. You could see and hear—and even smell—evidence of a new Leavenworth being born. Excitement radiated throughout the town!

Cranes and other equipment assaulted the buildings. Scaffolding rose up from the street level to the new roofs. Workmen were everywhere, clambering up the sides and over the roofs of the buildings. Tourists and sidewalk superintendents watched the entire show from the comfort of the city park on the other side of the street. As Pauline said, "Sidewalk superintending is becoming almost a full-time job!" What a wonderful sight it was to see more smiles on people's faces, wide-eyed looks of anticipation, even childlike delight in the magic of what was unfolding.

Some people were seeing Old European architecture and decorative motifs for the first time—stucco and half-timbering; Old World wrought iron, light fixtures and specially carved woodwork; small, artistic wooden signs and Old European art. Workers came from Leavenworth, nearby Cashmere and other towns. Out on the street you could watch Ferd Sorensen teach woodworking techniques to the carpenters and workmen.

Enthusiasm seemed to mount every day! People were beginning to get into the swing of tourism, and the spirit of cooperation was strong enough to create a new image for Leavenworth.

Bob and I were excited when we received Earl's designs for our buildings. Situated at the bend of Front Street, the Tannenbaum was a natural focal point downtown. It was to become the Tannenbaum Gift Shop (which has since moved to a new location on Front Street). In the gable of the roof we installed a glockenspiel, and the building became a showcase for photographers.

Chuck Bowen built the clockworks, and Kit Clark designed and carved the colorful wooden and animated dancing figures. Every hour on the hour, the glockenspiel doors open and two Bavarian couples dance around underneath the clock. The glockenspiel is synchronized to perform on the hour while the village carillon bells ring out different tunes.

Bob and I wanted to build a large Old Bavarian-style overhanging roof on the Tannenbaum Building, and this required us to ask the city for a vacation of a portion of sidewalk on Front Street. The Universal Building Code stated that a roof or balcony could overhang a sidewalk no more than four feet—a major obstacle for us because a Bavarian roof often had an overhang of six, eight or more feet. Also, we were required to use fire retardant materials. Little did we realize the city would take several months to study our vacation request—even to hold hearings on it—before they would give us an answer.

Our plans involved relocating the main entrance of the building under a massive arch to face the whole town, and they involved murals by a local German artist, Al Wierich. Another artist, Herb Schraml, was brought in from Seattle by Heinz Ulbricht to paint murals on the Edelweiss Hotel and the two Herrett buildings. Eventually Herb moved to Leavenworth, and today his beautiful work may be seen on the outside walls of several other buildings in town, as well as inside Cafe Christa, the Danish bakery and other establishments.

During this period, Bob and I had been working very closely with Cliff Hedeen, of Bothell, Washington. Cliff was an expert at wood carving, and in 1966 he made signs for our buildings, ornamental plaques and the brightly colored wooden benches outside the Tannenbaum Gift Shop. The following year we asked him to design and build the big "Willkommen zu Leavenworth"

Art in the Park made its debut in the summer of 1966. LaVerne Peterson (standing with painting), Ann and Vern Herrett (seated at table) and I confer. In the background, LaVerne's remodeled Edelweiss Hotel (left) and the two Herrett buildings are nearing completion.

Jorgen's Danish Bakery opened just before Leavenworth received the 1968 All America City Award. John Espelund and his right-hand helper, Vi Rembold, serve coffee and pastry to the local "kaffeeklatsch," gathered at the round table to catch up on the local news. Cal and Arleen Blackburn, in Bavarian attire for a festival weekend, sit at John's right.

sign motorists see when entering town. Cliff continued to design signs for Leavenworth merchants for many years.

Another thing we had to plan for was special lighting effects such as Christmas lights and flood lights. They would require the installation of many outside electrical outlets at the Tannenbaum Building. For the electrical work, we hired Chuck Bowen without opening the job to other bidders. Although Chuck did an excellent job, this proved to be a blunder on my part. Frankly, I gave the electrical work on our two buildings to Chuck to win him over to tourism. All too late I realized my mistake. It was unfair to Owen Watson, the other leading electrician in Leavenworth, and I have always regretted the slight to Owen, especially in light of the hard times he and his wife Pauline had endured and Pauline's leadership in Project Alpine.

Despite the setbacks and mistakes, each day brought a new wave of excitement, and in turn more cooperation among Leavenworth's citizens. Even so, a few old timers were resentful, even angry, that their town was undergoing such radical changes. And some merchants showed signs of envy. As outsiders, Bob and I frequently were scapegoats for these feelings.

Some of the criticism leveled at me took a humorous bent. My old blue station wagon had "The Squirrel Tree" painted on it, and I was back and forth from the restaurant to Leavenworth several times a day. My coming and going gave rise to this poem which appeared in *The Echo*:

ALPINEITIS

We live in a town, not so very big in girth,
The name of this town is at present Leavenworth.
It was a nice quiet town, 'cept for feudin' o'er a school.
And we even had our own community swimming pool.
Now an Alpine bee came a-buzzin' into town.
And he stung the folks to action so they can't sit down.
They're all nervously competing
(call it co-operation, by the way)
And their bank rolls they're depleting,
While they try to act so gay.
Now it's Alpine this, and Alpine that—
Even our Alpine dog chases an Alpine cat.

And our Edelweiss cows are giving goat's milk cheese,
While an Alpine frog yodels in the Alpine breeze.
Soon the tourists will be climbing
Up our Mountain Home Alps,
While the Old Timers sit and scratch their Alpineized scalps.
Well, now, I tell you folks, that I've had it "up to here."
So I'm going into town and get an Alpine beer!

By Alpine-nonamous

P.S. I wouldn't dare to sign my name—I'd be labeled as a foe,
And end up in a sad disgrace
With the Bavarians, and gestapo.
But I think it's still the U.S.A.,
With the freedom of the Press—
And I think some folks will (secretly) side with me—
Or do I miss my guess?

As we knew would happen, the media—especially the newspapers in Wenatchee, Seattle and Spokane focused on Leavenworth and provided a great deal of free publicity. Indeed, the entire state of Washington was beginning to hear about Leavenworth. In the summer of 1966 *The Seattle Times* gave us excellent coverage with a front-page story and a large color photograph. More free publicity followed, and soon articles began appearing in out-of-state newspapers. When time permitted, I also made publicity contacts with the media and with people in state government.

By the fall of 1966, inquiries about establishing new businesses were being made from as far away as the Midwest. Yet in those early months of construction, we had often watched in frustration as cars drove right through town without stopping. The hoped-for tourists slowed down to watch the building activity on Front Street and some even satisfied their curiosity by walking around the scaffolding, but they all soon continued on their way. Within a few years, however, hundreds of thousands of visitors would be arriving in this miracle town!

THE BEAUTIFICATION PROGRAM—
CLEANING UP LEAVENWORTH

"Out of the new building developments came this wonderful enthusiasm and cooperation, where it wasn't only just the adults that got involved, but even the school! We had a marvelous clean-up, where all the high school kids got involved. And it was very contagious! Virtually everyone in the community got into the spirit of the thing, because they could see what a beautiful town was developing here. It even went out into the community where the people were cleaning up their yards, sprucing up their houses, painting—everything!"

— *Daphne Clark*

The generally depressed atmosphere of Leavenworth in the 1960s pervaded both the business and residential areas. Many downtown buildings were poorly maintained and although front entrances might be clean, garbage and other debris were piled in the alleyways. At Eighth and Commercial streets the city was using a vacant lot to store snow plows and other equipment.

In the residential areas, junk was piled everywhere. Broken-down cars, refrigerators, children's toys and countless other items could be found on driveways, lawns and front porches.

Bob and I had talked about these eyesores a great deal, between ourselves and with community leaders. We knew there had to be a general clean-up, but the city didn't have a nickel to spend on it. In discussing the idea with Russ Lee, publisher of *The Echo*, we realized that if we were going to suggest a cleanup to anybody else, we should begin with our own places!

As our first move to spruce up the town, we invited the volunteer firemen to burn down two of our delapidated, empty rental houses—for practice. Next, with Bob Brender's help we removed a number of broken down commercial signs along the highway coming into town, some of which advertised businesses that no longer existed.

In 1967, after Dick Stroup was elected president of the chamber of commerce and I was elected vice president, we discussed a general cleanup and beautification of the town. This project became a top priority for Dick while he was in office—in fact, both Dick and his wife Rena have guided several beautification projects in Leavenworth.

Dick and I saw eye-to-eye on many things, but he made one decision to which I objected strongly and on which I was proven dead wrong: the appointment of E. L. (Shag) Coffin as chairman of the Beautification Committee. Shag turned out to be the perfect choice for this job. He went to the high school with a chamber-sponsored program in which each class competed to bring in the most trash.

These young people were terrific! They collected junk and deposited it in 50 x 100 foot piles along Highway 2 near downtown. These mountains of debris contained some 400 wrecked cars and many refrigerators, rusty bedsprings and other discarded items.

Russ and Vera Lee launched the clean-up drive with a lead article in their *Echo*, and—with their children Tom, Carolyn and Sally—supported the project wholeheartedly. Russ and I went out around town photographing business locations and private properties where junk and trash lay abandoned—beginning with our own buildings! Russ printed a number of these pictures in the next issue of *The Echo*, along with the headline, "One Big Junk Yard!" We intended to point a finger at ourselves as well as others.

Our first community cleanup had been a big success and each spring thereafter, when the snow was gone, some of the merchants and their families got together to sweep the downtown sidewalks and streets of winter's accumulated debris.

~ 7 ~

The Remodeling Continues

"When I came to Leavenworth it was a very depressed town. And the attitude of the people was depressed. You'd see them walking down the street, their heads hanging down, and not looking happy. And it was a drab place, even though there was so much beauty surrounding it. As these buildings started developing, I would see these people walking along, their heads in the air, and a smile on their faces! Same people that a year before hadn't looked like there was ever a future for them!"
— *Daphne Clark*

While the first six buildings were being completed, construction of the next six remodeling projects began and now many others were caught up in the enthusiasm. The six new projects were:

1. The Barber Shop Building, owned by Chuck and Vera Bergman and designed by Heinz Ulbricht. Chuck's special interest was the Leavenworth Ski Jumps, which occurred every fourth year when Leavenworth played host to the National Ski Jumping competition. Because of this interest, Chuck hired Herb Schraml to paint a mural depicting the jumps on the Barber Shop Building. Then, at eye level, in a front wall niche, Chuck placed a large woodcarving of a ski jumper holding his skis.

2. Larsen Drug Store, owned by Enoch and Evelyn Larsen and designed by Heinz Ulbricht. The Larsens hired a local contractor, Lloyd Ward, to do the remodeling.

3. The Seattle First National Bank, designed by Heinz Ulbricht and remodeled under the direction of the bank's new manager, Ray Alvarez.

4. The Corner Supply Building, owned by Dale and Barbara Seaman. Even though they were financially unable to make major renovations, the

Chamber of Commerce Presidents during the early years of Leavenwoth's revitalization: (from left) Bob Brender, 1965-66; Dick Stroup, 1967; me, 1968; Archie Marlin, 1969; Rod Simpson, 1970; (not pictured) Owen Watson, 1971.

Seamans wanted to show their support, so they installed Old German wood facings to the front of their building.

5. City Hall (repainted).

6. The Bandstand, which was completed in 1968.

Leavenworth Chamber of Commerce—1966 Officers

I knew that 1966 would be the make-or-break year for us, and the chamber presidency was a vital position for keeping things on track. Bob Brender, who had always been strongly supportive, was ready to step down as president, yet we needed him to stay on because he was familiar with the details of all our plans for tourism and remodeling.

Often the first vice-president of the chamber ascended to the leadership, but at that time, the office was held by Frank Motteler, who declined because of health problems and because he felt he wasn't sufficiently up to date on all chamber projects.

Likewise, the second vice-president, Dick Stroup, indicated he was not yet ready to step into the presidency, although he looked forward to it the following year.

Bob finally agreed to stay on another year even though, unknown to us, he was going through a painful personal dilemma. When Bob was absent from chamber meetings, Dick Stroup gradually took over more and more. Bob Rodgers and I were both board members, and during this somewhat awkward time, we tried to be as helpful to Dick as we could. In 1967 Dick was elected chamber president. Then and always, Dick Stroup and his wife Rena contributed greatly to all aspects of the revitalization of Leavenworth.

The Bank Goes Alpine

Back in 1961, when Bob and I had been building The Squirrel Tree Chalet Motel, we fell short of funds and needed $3,500 to pay the overrun on construction costs. To my amazement, the Leavenworth branch of the Seattle First National Bank refused our request for a loan. Partly because of this experience, I wanted to help building owners obtain loans for remodeling from the bank.

As soon as the Alpine remodeling plan was approved, I arranged a visit to the bank's Seattle headquarters. Bob Rodgers, Pauline Watson and I were very pleased with the warm reception we received and with the spirit of cooperation that developed.

Later Heinz Ulbricht talked to Seattle First about doing the design for the remodeling of its Leavenworth bank building. He drew up an excellent design and offered to be the contractor—all for a very reasonable fee.

The local bank manager, Ray Alvarez, was definitely "pro-Alpine" and as construction on the first six buildings was nearing completion, his reports to the main office helped persuade Seattle First to adopt the Bavarian theme for its Leavenworth branch. From then on Ray helped the local owners in every way he could.

Pauline Watson remembers teasing him about it: "I remember the day so well, the day that we took the scaffolding down. The building was done...and Ray

"I can well remember when Ted and Bob and I would sit and talk, and one of their great concerns, especially Ted's great concern, was (when) we got over the initial enthusiasm with the first five or six buildings then what was going to happen? Would we fall off? Would the whole thing kind of fall apart at that point? What kind of follow up were we going to have? It was a concern, and it has been all through the years.

Another stumbling block was financing, as it was going to be with any town. A town that's dying? Who's going to lend money to do some fancy building?"

— Pauline Watson

The Seattle First National Bank goes Bavarian. Top left. The bank in 1965. Top right. Construction is well underway. Bottom left and right. Herb Schraml painted the first mural on the building. A later mural was done by Cordi Bradburn. In 1996 the Huntington Boyd family purchased the building and enlarged and remodeled it once again.

Alverez was standing out in the street...and I said 'Ray, if this doesn't work, you may be the first banker of Seattle First National to own a whole town!'"

A Trip to Europe

By late 1966 the vision for our town was becoming an exciting reality, but instead of having a proud sense of accomplishment I was seriously troubled. Bob and I were deeply in debt and facing possible bankruptcy. Our collateral was our mortgaged restaurant and motel and smaller pieces of real estate for which there were still no buyers. Unwisely, perhaps, we had continued to buy more properties.

We mortgaged everything we owned to remodel the Tannenbaum Building and we were in hock to the hilt. We seemed forever to be negotiating for more loans—to meet the payments on real estate purchases; to meet the payroll at the restaurant and the new Tannenbaum Gift Shop; to pay for maintenance expenses, taxes and insurance and to purchase equipment, supplies and merchandise for our businesses.

With our expanded role in Leavenworth affairs, we had let The Squirrel Tree and Chalet Motel business slide. The first year gross daily sales at the Tannenbaum Gift Shop in Leavenworth were often as low as $6 or $7 a day. As with many a new business, we used a lot of red ink in the books. At the time we seemed headed for financial disaster and, in fact, it would be a couple of years before the gift shop showed any significant profit.

We were especially concerned that with all our pleading for authenticity, we ourselves might be the ones who wouldn't be able to afford the additional costs involved. What a humiliating irony it would be if we were the first to go belly up! Would it be a forewarning that the Leavenworth Bavarian village dream might be a failure?

Bob seemed to handle the pressure and frustration better than I. Personally, I often wondered if I might be headed for a nervous breakdown. In order to reduce the stress, we decided to close The Squirrel Tree in September 1966, well ahead of our normal winter closure. And then, unbelieveably, another miraculous thing occurred. An angel appeared in the person of Carolyn Schutte.

Actually, Bob and I first came to know Carolyn and her husband Carl as regular customers at The Squirrel Tree. If Carolyn had a former life, it must have been as royalty. Her whole bearing was that of a very gracious, lovable queen. She enjoyed beautiful things and places, including her home on the shore of Lake Washington in Seattle's Windermere district.

Carolyn and Carl liked what we were doing at Cole's Corner, and they were generous in their praise. It was Carl who first suggested we build a motel next door, and when he passed on, Carolyn frequently brought guests to The Squirrel Tree Chalet Motel. On those occasions when I shared with her my vision of an authentic Bavarian community, she never waivered in her enthusiasm or encouragement, saying, "a right idea cannot help but succeed."

The Huntington Boyd Building, formerly the Icicle Tavern (left) is transformed.

Above. Carolyn Schutte and her beloved St. Bernard puppy, Wendy, at our Leavenworth home. Below. On our trip to Europe we visit Bavaria where Bob Rodgers (left) presents The Leavenworth Echo 1966 Sunshine Edition *to the burgermeister (or mayor) of Oberammergau, Herr Winke.*

Carolyn became a very good friend to Bob and me. She was wise and compassionate, yet she could be stern. One aspect of life we shared was our spiritual values. We were not openly religious people in the usual ways, yet we each held firm, deep convictions about the sanctity of all life and the oneness of all peoples.

As our friendship grew, Carolyn invited Bob and me to be guests in her Seattle home, and she visited Leavenworth more frequently. One day she invited me over to talk—to find out how things were going—and talk we did! Along with our financial problems, I felt swamped with a variety of activities, current and future. My days seemed a strange and unsettling mix of enthusiasm and depression. The gratifying sense of watching the vision unfold was often clouded by the hopelessness with which I viewed our financial state.

I was also deeply disturbed by the seeming lack of appreciation by some of the merchants and townspeople and by gossip about me and Bob, some of which was quite malicious. To this latter concern Carolyn said, "You've just got to love them—love them to death!" At another time she had said, "Now, Ted, when you get up in the morning, the first thing you must do is grease your ears and let all this gossip pass right on through. Pay no attention to it. Do not take this into your consciousness." And sometimes at breakfast she would ask, "Have you greased your ears good this morning?"

But on this occasion, after I spoke awhile, Carolyn looked at me and said, "Well, the town doesn't appreciate you, but I do....Now I know why I came here. God sent me to assist in your endeavors." She told me plainly that I was carrying the weight of the world on my shoulders and that I simply had to turn loose from it all for awhile. Yes, but how? I saw no way out. Not only did I have extensive commitments in Leavenworth, we had huge financial obligations.

Carolyn then announced that she had decided to lend Bob and me enough money to see us through our current financial problems, as well as enough to buy the much-needed quality European merchandise for the Tannenbaum Gift Shop. And, she emphasized, she did not care if we ever paid her back. Bob and I were completely dumbfounded!

But she wasn't finished. She shocked us by calmly stating she was going to take Bob and me to Europe, with all our expenses paid. This, she said, would enable us to buy the European merchandise we needed firsthand, and it would be an excellent opportunity to study Bavarian and Old World architecture and countless other design features useful in creating Bavarian Leavenworth. Also, she felt the trip would give us both a good rest.

On that day, our lives were forever altered, thanks to Carolyn Schutte. This European trip marked a major change in our lives. Suddenly, as if by magic, we were relieved of the threat of bankruptcy. Moreover, we had talked for months about how, if we only could afford it, we would go to Europe. Even though we attended trade shows in America, there were some items that were available only in Europe. Now we could offer quality European merchandise in our new gift shop that people couldn't find anywhere in the region—and at a very low price.

We left for Europe in October, flew to Copenhagen, then motored down through Europe. It was a whirlwind tour that lasted more than a month. From Denmark to Bavaria, we traveled through Germany, Lichtenstein, Belgium, France, Switzerland and Austria. Among other things, we revisited one of Bob's favorite places, Mittenwald, in the heart of Bavaria, where he had photographed several buildings in 1955.

I took hundreds of photographs—of architectural styles, design and decorative features, roofs and windows, flower boxes, doorknobs and people, especially when they appeared in traditional Bavarian costume. Heinz Ulbricht had asked us to bring back illustrations of bandstands, since he had agreed to design one for the city park in Leavenworth. I did so, but they all proved to be much too ornate for our town. I also brought back pictures of a small old covered bridge at Lucerne, Switzerland—an ideal model for a smaller bridge we wanted to build to Blackbird Island in Leavenworth.

We also visited Oberammergau, site of the famous Passion Play, because one of my dreams was that Leavenworth and Oberammergau become sister cities. (This dream has not materialized—at least as of this writing.)

Before embarking on our trip, we got a letter of introduction from Leavenworth Mayor Wilbur Bon. However, when Carolyn, Bob and I met with Oberammergau mayor, or Burgermeister, Herr Winke, we discovered he didn't speak English. Although Bob had a passable command of German, our meeting might not have been very productive but, as it turned out, Carolyn was quite fluent in the language so she conducted the meeting, translating for both parties.

"I probably would have to say that all during this time, from when we first conceived the idea for Leavenworth and probably for several years after, I just didn't see how we were going to afford it. How were we going to pay for it? I was the one that was probably dragging my feet. The cost of remodelling by today's standards was a pittance, but in those days it was a tremendous amount of money. And I didn't see how we could do it. And we almost didn't. We just about went bankrupt! And we practically bankrupted our minds at the same time. It was mind boggling—all this money we owed, and we didn't see any way of paying for it."

— Bob Rodgers

The top photos on these two pages show the Fitz Building (left) and Chuck and Vera Bergman's Barber Shop Building (right) before and after remodeling. (Note Herb Schraml's colorful mural of ski jumps.) The Fitz Building was remodeled by Heinz Ulbricht and Joe Jackson, while Heinz designed the Barber Shop Building. Bottom photos, left to right. Three views of the Fitz Building during and after remodeling. A carved wooden ski jumper greets passersby from his niche in the facade of the Barber Shop Building which later housed the Wood Shop. Lower right. Barber Chuck Bergman at work.

The old Shelton Cafe Building was owned by LaVerne Peterson and sold to Emery Wechselberger, who remodeled it into the Hotel Tyrol. The building houses a variety of shops at street level.

The Don Hansen family purchased this old building, tore it down, and recently built the new Leavenworth Brewery, which has a commanding position in the village.

The old Gateway Shell Station in 1965. Annette Hart and Dick and Rena Stroup transformed it to Bavarian style in 1967. After a fire nearly destroyed the building, it was again remodeled to become Gustav's.

The Yes Sir Chevrolet Garage on the corner of Ninth and Commercial Street is now the Obertal Mall.

Der Markt Platz, the most authentic of the five buildings Bob and I remodeled. Above. Early photographs of the building before reconstruction in 1977, when we removed the roof and entire front of the building. From lower far left, steel beams are installed to support the added second floor and new roof. Masons create the appearance of half-timbering by applying stucco to the outside brick walls, and (this page, left) the rear of the building, before and after its transformation.

Bavarian Leavenworth is true to Old World models. Balconies and roofs project out over sidewalks, walls feature Alpine murals, flowers cascade from baskets and tubs, and handpainted signs and old-fashioned shop windows entice passersby.

While we were in Europe, we bought a variety of gift items to sell in our shop. Of special note were wood carvings from Oberammergau, decorated cow bells from Switzerland, leather purses from Dinkersbühl, wooden plates from Austria, Tyrolean hats from Austria and lederhosen from Bavaria. We also bought Bavarian dress suits hand-tailored at Loden-Frey, the famous department store in Munich. A few years later the Royal Bavarian organization was formed in Leavenworth, and these suits gave its members ideas for their official dress.

Above. Dick and Rena Stroup's Plumbing Shop is remodeled and becomes A Book For All Seasons.

What a blessing it was to be away from what had become an intense and pressured life in Leavenworth. And how grateful I was to have over a month free of committee meetings! We returned not only with new merchandise and countless photographs, but with new lives and renewed energy. And we owed it all to Carolyn Schutte.

Over the years, Carolyn was helpful to me in countless other ways. As a Christian Scientist, she practiced the healing principles taught by Mary Baker Eddy, and with Carolyn's help I was finally able to quit smoking. For many years I had been such a heavy cigarette and pipe smoker I even smoked my pipe in the shower. I simply turned it upside down rather than remove it from my mouth! I had tried to quit several times, but nothing seemed to work.

One day, on a drive from Leavenworth to Wenatchee, I casually told Carolyn of my desire to quit. "Well," she said, "would you like for me to treat for you?" I wasn't sure what she really meant, but I suspected she referred to spiritual healing. Somewhat uneasy, I thought I'd just go along with her and said, "Okay, that would be nice."

"Now don't expect anything right away," she said, "it may be six months or more, but one day you'll just leave your cigarettes and pipe on the table and

Opposite. The transformation of Front Street looking east through time as old Leavenworth is revitalized to become a prosperous Bavarian village.

97

never pick them up again. Nor will you have any desire for them again, whatsoever." Carolyn said this in a quiet, matter-of-fact manner, and then she did something bewildering. She went right out and bought me a brand new pipe! In less than three months precisely what she said would happen did happen. And I've never again had the desire to smoke.

The Bandstand

In 1965, at one of the morning coffee sessions in the Tumwater Cafe, I suggested to Vern Herrett and Bob Brender, then chamber president, that we build a bandstand. Many small towns are built around a town square that becomes the focal point for gatherings of all kinds. Leavenworth does not have a town square; instead, the center of the village is the downtown park. In the early years the park contained a bandstand, but it had been removed long before we arrived in Leavenworth.

Later, we discussed the idea on the Project Alpine committee. The reason I suggested a bandstand was the popularity of the non-stop Bavarian band music we played at The Squirrel Tree and my feeling that the town needed a focal point for entertainment.

While everyone wanted the bandstand, there was no money for the city to build one. But in 1966 Carolyn Schutte said she wanted to donate $1,000 to Leavenworth for any project the town wanted and asked us for a suggestion. We responded that a bandstand would be an ideal addition to Bavarian Leavenworth.

At a chamber meeting in July 1966, Carolyn presented her check to the city and the bandstand project was launched. Immediately, other individuals and organizations came forward with donations of time and money. The Vesta Junior Women's Club gave about $1,000 from its Sears prize money, many people volunteered to help build the bandstand and Joan James did a wonderful job organizing the volunteers.

Heinz Ulbricht had never before designed a bandstand, but with the help of pictures from our European trip and from Solvang he drew up a design for $250. Newell and Nancy Arntson brought in a sound system at cost, then provided free installation and maintenance. Some of the women of

Top. The new bandstand under construction in the Downtown City Park. Bottom. One morning many volunteers came to roll out new sod for the park and accidently covered up all the sprinklers. That afternoon embarrassed workers had to search under the sod to uncover the sprinklers! Sod-detectives pictured here are (from lower left) John Rogers, Morris McKenzie, Louie Sneider, Chuck Langlois, Joe Rinke and Bob Rodgers.

Leavenworth volunteered to landscape the bandstand area. The entire project cost the town a little over $5,000. The bandstand (now referred to as a gazebo) has proven to be everything everyone hoped it would be. Music groups of all kinds from many parts of the country have performed there throughout the year, to the enjoyment of throngs of visitors.

All America City Award

In 1966, given the outstanding success of Leavenworth's revitalization, Bob Brender and I discussed applying for *LOOK Magazine's* All America City Award. When *LOOK Magazine* began sponsoring the annual All America City Award to honor the cities where citizen involvement had resolved major local urban ills, it did so in the belief that "The concern and involvement of ordinary citizens is our best—perhaps our only—hope of solving the serious crises facing our cities today."

Ken Nyberg, Project LIFE counselor, however, advised that we should wait at least until the following year. We took his advice, and during the summer of 1967 chamber secretary Hazel Hansen and I spent some 100 hours preparing the application.

When Leavenworth was chosen to be among the top finalists, we were invited to send a delegation to Milwaukee, Wisconsin, to make a final presentation. Pauline Watson and Bob Rodgers were appointed to go, and Hazel was asked to assist them. Their trip to Milwaukee was financed by various contributions: we passed the hat at the next chamber meeting; Archie Marlin sold hot peanut brittle in the city park; members of the Tamarack Womens

ALL AMERICA CITY
LEAVENWORTH, WA.

"The winning cities are distinguished by that extra spark of honest openness that encourages hometown people to care, to act, and to prove — particularly in this year of simmering urban tension — that Americans can still live together productively and peacefully."
— *LOOK Magazine, April 16, 1968*

During its trip to Milwaukee to make the final presentation for the 1967 All America City Award, the Leavenworth delegation stops over in the Swiss theme town of New Glarus, Wisconsin. Left to right. Chamber secretary Hazel Hansen, chamber president, Dick Stroup, presenters Bob Rodgers and Pauline Watson, Swiss flag thrower Roger Bright, Rena Stroup, and the group's New Glarus hostess.

Club had a rummage and white elephant sale and still other organizations and individuals gave money. Chamber president Dick Stroup and his wife Rena accompanied the Leavenworth three to Milwaukee, paying their own expenses and arranging the Leavenworth display.

The awards were announced early in 1968, after I had become president of the chamber; but when the chamber secretary received the letter from *LOOK Magazine* announcing that we had won an award, I was not informed. I learned of the presentation from Russ Lee, editor of *The Echo*, who was of course astounded that I as chamber president didn't know.

Ironically, while we were being recognized as a town that exemplified teamwork, undercurrents of discord were becoming more and more evident. I myself had felt the resentment of a few old timers so strongly I had submitted my resignation as chamber president shortly after I was elected. Although Archie Marlin and others persuaded me to continue in that office, I remained troubled by the attempts of some individuals to tell the story of Leavenworth's revitalization in fanciful ways. Essential elements of what happened were being left out of the official accounts, and people who had little or nothing to do with creating Bavarian Leavenworth were starting to be named as responsible. Local pride and enthusiasm sometimes crossed over the line of integrity, and soon new facts about the revitalization were being invented to give recognition to a few old timers. This was deeply disturbing to me, so I went to Russ Lee and asked him to use a special headline in the 1968 Sunshine Edition of *The Echo*: "Leavenworth—God's Miracle!" It was high time, truly, to give credit squarely where it belonged.

Design Review Board

From 1965 to 1970 there were no legal guidelines or restrictions that compelled building owners to follow the Bavarian theme or bound anyone to remodel in an authentic way. Yet we enjoyed the complete cooperation of building owners in every aspect of design and construction. I don't know of a major instance when, to save money, an owner looked for a way to avoid maintaining a high quality of Bavarian design. That was to happen later, after we had a design review board!

However, we did have some trouble defining what we meant by "authentic Bavarian design." When we told those involved in construction that we wanted to create a Bavarian village that looked to be over 100 years old, the questions most often asked were "What is Bavarian?" and "What is authentic among all the various 'Bavarian' designs and motifs?"

In the spring of 1968 Mayor Wilbur Bon appointed Bob Rodgers to define "Bavarian" and to make preliminary recommendations for a design review board. Bob was to consider designs for all architecture, signs, decorative motifs and other details, including exterior building design, signs, building materials, lighting and other features.

Bob contacted the University of Washington for assistance. He wrote letters to Palm Springs and to Carmel, Solvang and other theme towns for information on setting up a review board. Many legal questions had be resolved before criteria could be established.

It took a couple of years for Leavenworth architect Rod Simpson and others to settle the legal aspects of the ordinances. Most of the problems involved sign restrictions, particularly those relating to interior signs that show up on the outsides of buildings and to all neon and illuminated signs. Finally, on July 16, 1970, the Leavenworth Design Review Board became official, although sign regulations did not become law until early 1971. Later, when revisions were needed, Karen Dean worked with others to draft amendments that appear in the present-day code.

Der Markt Platz

In 1973 we bought what is probably Leavenworth's most prominent building, at the corner of Front and Eighth Streets. At the time it housed the Corner Supply Hardware store. In January 1974 we had sold the Tannenbaum Gift Shop to Russell and Vera Lee so that after selling *The Leavenworth Echo* to Earl Petersen they could continue to make a living in Leavenworth.

To help Heinz Ulbricht create a design for our new building, we gave him our slides of Bavaria and drew his attention to those of Garmisch-Partenkirchen. The slides showed clearly the big overhanging roofs, wide overhanging balconies, flowerboxes and other features we wanted him to incorporate in his design.

At first we rejected all of Heinz's designs as not being authentic enough, but later we told him we were willing to gut the building and add a second story to achieve a more authentic look. Eventually we agreed on a design that suited our tastes very well, one we could accept in spite of the large additional expense of adding another floor. However, as we were soon to discover, the city building code would not permit construction. It was a problem we and other building owners had encountered before, and now we decided the code would simply have to be changed.

By the late 1970s the city council was receiving a transfusion of new blood, especially in the person of Andy Pashkowski. A man of the highest integrity, Andy always carefully considered both sides to every issue presented to the council, and it was Andy who removed the barriers to changing the building codes. Before the end of that year, Heinz and I went to the council and explained that to appear truly Old Bavarian, balconies and roofs should overhang the sidewalk by much more than four feet.

LEAVENWORTH BAVARIAN HOMES

As I envisioned Bavarian Leavenworth, there would be Bavarian-styled homes in the residential areas. In particular, Bob and I were interested in Hobo Gulch, a stretch of some twenty-four acres along the Wenatchee River. In 1965 Bob and I bought this land for $500 an acre with the intention of eventually building Bavarian houses on it. (Bob always said that lumber costs were just as much for an attractive Bavarian-style home as they were for a box-like one.) We asked Heinz

Ulbricht and an engineering firm to plat the land and then changed the name to Bayern Village.

In 1966 Carolyn Schutte decided she was going to build a house at Bayern Village, and she asked Bob and me to work with Heinz to design it in the Bavarian style. Because of the high cost of developing the property, however, the house was never built. We later sold Bayern Village and the new owners took over the development of Bavarian homes there.

In 1970 we purchased some acreage on Mountain Home, a beautiful ridge across from downtown Leavenworth that is covered with pine trees and a kaleidoscope of spring flowers and has outstanding views of the Leavenworth valley and the mountains. In the early 1970s I worked with Bob Johnson and Heinz on the designs for what was to be the second of two Bavarian houses in the Leavenworth area and then with Bob and Nola Johnson on the construction. In later years, Bob Johnson, Vern Peterson and others built more Bavarian houses.

The council agreed not to restrict balconies and roofs as long as they didn't interfere with street traffic, such as large trucks, or create some other safety problem. With these basic changes in the city building codes approved, other building owners could begin remodeling in a more thoroughly authentic Bavarian style.

The new approved design for our building was finished in February 1977. It included the addition of a second story, five-foot wide balconies running the length of the building on Front and Eighth streets and a massive roof extending over these balconies another two or three feet. (In 1978, to our surprise, Ray and Beverly Baker who owned Norris Hardware across Eighth Street from Der Markt Platz, added two floors instead of one and still stayed within the 50-foot height restrictions.)

Before construction on our building could begin, however, the old roof and the entire front of the building had to be removed. Steel beams then had to be installed to carry the heavy commercial traffic anticipated on the second floor. To overcome the hazard of ice and snow on the roof, we installed snow guards along the roof edges and electrical wires to melt the snow.

We named our building Der Markt Platz, the Market Place, and in time it housed a very interesting gift shop. Heinz Ulbricht and his wife Christa leased space on the second floor, where they opened an authentic German restaurant, Cafe Christa. Flower boxes and tables lined both balconies, where outdoor dining was featured. The lease agreement we drew up required that fresh flowers be used on all the tables.

Bob Rodgers and I added two other shops: Kris Kringle, a Christmas store, and The Yum Yum Tree, a candy shop. (Kris Kringle is now owned by Carl Evans and is located on Front Street.)

Other Improvements

During this time, another problem facing Bavarian Leavenworth was solved: the massive power and telephone poles that filled the alleys behind the buildings and the maze of wires that obstructed views were quietly placed underground. Although the town could not bear the expense of burying these utilities, the Chelan County P.U.D. and General Telephone did the job and in the process greatly improved everyone's view of the mountains and the valley.

~ 8 ~

Festivals
and
Entertainment

"... let's put Leavenworth on the map as the biggest little art center in the state!"

— Archie Marlin

"Leavenworth, that Bavaria-inspired jewel of Washington State's Cascade Mountains, has become a favorite autumn tourist attraction....By the car and bus load, until the last bright leaf flutters down, visitors will be converging on the little Icicle Creek town which pulled itself up by its boot straps a few years ago and emerged as an 'all-America city' much honored in national civic improvement competition."

— The Seattle Post-Intelligencer, September 23, 1973

Over the years Leavenworth has hosted a number of seasonal festivals and special events. Currently these include: Art in the Park, the Bavarian Ice Fest, Mai Fest, Craft Fair, Kinderfest, the International Folk Dance Performance, the Wenatchee River Salmon Festival, the Washington State Autumn Leaf Festival, the Leavenworth Accordian Celebration, the Square Dance Weekend, the Leavenworth Gala Holiday Food Fair and the Christmas Lighting Festival.

Bob and I were involved in establishing three of the biggest annual festival celebrations in Leavenworth: the Washington State Autumn Leaf Festival, Christmas Lighting and Mai Fest, and we worked behind the scenes to bring forth Art in the Park.

Washington State Autumn Leaf Festival

The first official celebration with autumn leaves was in 1964, and this initiated perhaps the most successful of all the Leavenworth festivals. Years before we started The Squirrel Tree, when Bob and I traveled through the area we were awestruck by the brilliant colors of vine maple, aspen and other foliage. We wondered why such magnificence and beauty weren't publicized and why more people didn't flock to the area to enjoy the grand display.

At The Squirrel Tree I discovered that people from Seattle and elsewhere took weekend drives into the mountains to see the brilliant autumn colors and that Stevens Pass had long been an unpublicized fall favorite of nature lovers and camera fans. For our part, Bob and I decorated The Squirrel Tree with boughs of colored leaves and began to publicize the fall foliage.

In the early 1960s, while hounding Washington newspaper offices for Highway 2 publicity, I occasionally talked with Wilfred R. Woods, publisher of *The Wenatchee Daily World*. Wilfred was a customer at The Squirrel Tree, and one day I was wondering aloud why more publicity wasn't out on the autumn leaves. Wilfred strongly reinforced the idea of creating an annual fall festival in Leavenworth to draw more people into the area and to give the media an event to publicize. I believe it was Wilfred who suggested we have a mature woman preside over the festivities as queen.

In my last June 1964 LIFE Tourism Committee meeting, I proposed an autumn leaf festival be held on two weekends—either the last two weeks in September, when the weather was relatively warm, or the last weekend of September and the first weekend of October, when the leaves had more color. Moreover, I thought we should give the festival three years to prove itself, and others later agreed to this suggestion.

Dick Stroup helps visitors during festival time by volunteering to man the Downtown City Park information booth.

At a subsequent meeting, Shirley Bowen took the leadership of a group to plan the first Autumn Leaf Festival, which was scheduled to coincide with the presentation of the Sears-Roebuck Foundation Award to the Vestas. Shirley and her husband Chuck did a wonderful job heading up the first festival programs, and her group quickly came under the temporary umbrella of the Leavenworth Chamber of Commerce. After the first successful festival, however, the group separated from the chamber to become the Washington State Autumn Leaf Festival, with Shirley Bowen as president,

Marion Speer as first vice president and me as second vice president. I also took on the publicity and promotion for this new group.

Two of the individuals most instrumental in Leavenworth's rebirth were Russell and Vera Lee, owners of *The Leavenworth Echo*. I didn't know Russ very well then, even though he occasionally joined Bob Brender, Vern Herrett and me for morning coffee at the Tumwater Cafe. However, I wanted to convince Russ to publish a special free edition of the paper, one designed to attract visitors to the area and to serve as Leavenworth's publicity brochure. It would include a feature article on the beauty of the autumn leaves, many photographs and a list of all the things to do in the Leavenworth area. At the time, I didn't know how many subscribers *The Echo* had, nor how many outsiders even saw it.

When Bob Brender and I went to *The Echo* office and proposed that Russ print a 10,000-copy special edition, his response was, "You guys are crazy!" We didn't know that his largest print run had been 1,000 copies. Once he got used to the idea, though, Russ said, "Sure. Why not—with some help." Later Russ told me, "...the longer we talked—you had it pretty well organized to start with. You had people lined up to write different articles on autumn leaves, fishing, mountain climbing, and all the wonderful activities. Vera was in charge of advertising, and you even went out with her and scoured the country to get advertising to pay for it."

When the 10,000 copies came off the press and had to be folded, high school students and adults volunteered for folding parties. Because there was as yet no widespread distribution of the paper, residents leaving town on business or pleasure were asked to take copies of the special edition with them to distribute.

These 10,000 copies disappeared instantly. Within a month I went back to Russ with the idea of printing a 25,000-copy color edition featuring the autumn leaves. Russ pointed out that his press couldn't print color and besides it was very expensive. Remembering the color photos of autumn leaves we'd already used in the Highway 2 booklet, I returned to Franklin Press in Yakima. They printed nearly 35,000 copies of that first color edition, all of which were distributed by the end of the year. That was the beginning in 1964 of what became the very successful *Sonnenschein*, or Sunshine Edition,

"They had a little semi-autumn leaf celebration there, right there at The Squirrel Tree,...before they even thought about the Autumn Leaf Festival."
— *Vi & Walt Rembld*

Michael McMahon and Vi Rembold greet visitors to Leavenworth's Four Seasons Recreation display at a Seattle exhibit. The display featured the Autumn Leaf Festival.

of *The Leavenworth Echo.* In 1996 the name was changed to *Sonnenschein auf Leavenworth: Visitor Guide.* From our "crazy print run" of 10,000 copies over thirty years ago, the *Visitor Guide,* printed in April and November, has a distribution of 200,000—and it is still free of charge.

The Sunshine Edition is definitely the best source of general information on everything the visitor wants to know about enjoying Leavenworth. It is available all over town and at various distribution points, including visitor information centers, throughout the Pacific Northwest and Western Canada. Naturally, it has become the most important publicity tool for Leavenworth, as well as a primary means of advertising for the business community. Although wide distribution outlets now exist, I still often carry bundles of this edition away with me when I leave town.

Besides helping launch the Sunshine Edition in 1964, I contacted newspapers and tv and radio stations, asking them to announce the festival, and I sent publicity releases throughout the state, particularly to the Puget Sound region, Seattle, Spokane and Wenatchee. Finally, I renewed my contacts with Nancy Davidson, Northwest editor of *Sunset Magazine,* a publication that had already given us some coverage.

One thing I really enjoyed doing in preparation for the festival was supplying fresh autumn leaves to decorate downtown. For twenty years, at festival time both Saturday mornings, I'd leave home before daybreak and drive along the back country roads collecting vine maple leaves from trees not visible from the roads. We displayed the leaves everywhere—on storefronts, sign posts and the street concession booths and in the city park. Vine maple leaves don't stay fresh or retain good color for more than two days, so they couldn't be cut before the weekend. Later on, as merchant demand for them grew, Chuck Langlois and others helped gather the leaves by the truckload.

The first Autumn Leaf Festival took place September 19-27, 1964 and was a total success! A tremendous crowd gathered in town, perhaps the largest ever outside the annual Leavenworth Championship Ski Jumps. I believe even Governor Albert Rossellini attended. The event was crowned by the presentation of the $10,000 Sears Award to the Vesta Junior Women's Club. There were thousands of people in town—and that was before a single Bavarian-style building was to be seen!

Today, a highlight of the festival is the Grand Parade, which takes place on the last Saturday of September and boasts dozens of floats and marching bands from towns all over the Pacific Northwest and Western Canada. In the original planning for the event, I followed Wilfred Woods' suggestion and proposed we elect a "Royal Lady," a woman of presence and maturity who had in some way given dedicated service to Leavenworth. The first Royal Lady was Martha Jensen.

The Royal Bavarians

The Leavenworth float in the Grand Parade was accompanied in the early years by men dressed in Leavenworth-style Bavarian attire—bright red jackets, colorful ties, lederhosen, Bavarian-style dress socks and hats with feathers. The men who volunteered for this event took care of their own expenses and evolved into a new group that became Leavenworth's goodwill ambassadors—the Royal Bavarians. They continued wearing this colorful attire for parades and changed to the traditional Bavarian suit for more formal occasions. The Royal Bavarians are responsible for covering their own expenses and serve throughout the year, welcoming groups who come to town from all over the world.

Below left. The Royal Bavarians, Leavenworth's goodwill ambassadors, extend a hearty "Willkommen zu Leavenworth." (Front row, from left) Lenard A. Smith, Bill Busse, Ron Hill, Bill Wells. (Back row, from left) Owen Watson, Dr. John Koenig, Jim Ward, Bob Cowan, Lynn Watson and Les Tiedeman.

Below. Forerunners of The Royal Bavarians, these volunteers wear lederhosen, red vests and ties as they assist visitors in town and accompany the Leavenworth float in parades and at special events. (From left) Mayor Wilbur Bon, Ted Simpson, Lynn Watson, Vera Lee (looking on), Russ Lee, Bob Rodgers, Heinz Ulbricht, an unidentified man, me, and Lenard A. Smith.

Christmas Lighting

Because of our experiences in—and enjoyment of—lighting the buildings at Merritt Inn in 1957 and again at Cole's Corner, Bob and I looked forward to a Christmas lights celebration for Leavenworth. The first Christmas Lighting Festival was held in 1966, but it had a few slow years before becoming the huge success it is today. Until 1981 the festival was held on a single weekend in December, but beginning that year the tremendous crowds required the chamber of commerce to add a second weekend. Now, Christmas Lighting is traditionally held on the first two weekends of December, although the ever-increasing crowds may make it necessary to add a third weekend.

For many Christmas celebrations, Dean and Wally Butzloff were Mr. and Mrs. Santa Claus. Sometimes they would arrive in town on a horse-drawn sleigh, sometimes by wagon, depending on the amount of snow we had. Once I think they came down from the sky in a helicopter! Sometimes they were attended by a couple of elves dressed as Santa's helpers.

In early December, Leavenworth can be a fairy-book town dusted with a light mantle of snow. When enough snow falls, cross-country and downhill skiing begin and horse-drawn sleigh rides are the order of the day. Leavenworth offers a variety of winter activities for every member of the family: cross-country skiing from the door of your motel, bed and breakfast or condominium; night-lighted family skiing near town and excellent downhill skiing roughly 35 miles away at Stevens Pass or Mission Ridge. Until a few years ago, Leavenworth enjoyed an international reputation for its 90-meter ski jumping hill, but successive winters of light snowfall forced the facility's near closure.

Even in winter, local and regional bands, choirs and dancing groups perform in the city park bandstand. Children build snowmen there and slide on their sleds and inner tubes.

Thick hot soups, baked apples, wursts, hot apple cider and other delicious food is sold from sidewalk stands. As a welcome convenience, bonfires are kept blazing on Front Street to warm visitors' cold hands and feet and a warming hut is available. When it is cold enough, people create ice sculptures and now

Archie Marlin volunteered to make his delicious peanut brittle at a Front Street stand. The sale of Archie's candies raised money for many worthy projects.

the town of Leavenworth hosts a Bavarian Ice Fest later each winter.

For many years our Danish baker, John Espelund, turned out thousands of Christmas goodies—traditional Yuletide cakes, cookies and breads and colorful gingerbread houses. John came to us from Denmark, via Canada and Solvang, where Bob and I first heard about his excellent skills. John seemed to fulfill our dream of opening a European bakery in Leavenworth, so we installed him in our newly remodeled Bakery Building.

John has a great sense of humor and always seems to greet life with gusto—to have a friendly handshake and a genuine smile for everyone. Soon after arriving in Leavenworth, he became "John, the Baker" to everyone and "the roundtable" at his bakery became the favorite gathering place.

John was very supportive of all activities that promised to improve Leavenworth. Now that John is retired, Beth Warman's Hansel and Gretel Restaurant and Mike's Bakery have become favored town meeting places.

One Christmas tradition that was introduced to Leavenworth by its German-born residents, particularly Ernie and Marianne Bielitzer, is the tradition of hanging an Advent wreath at the entrance to each shop. These wreaths have four lights, each of which is lit on succeeding weeks in December until by Christmas Day all four are lit. The lights signify the advent of Christ's birth.

One of many decorations Bob and I had each year was a very large Christmas tree covered with thousands of 'hot pink' lights. We set up the tree on the sidewalk outside of Der Markt Platz—right in the center of town. Inevitably, just before Christmas someone would steal the whole tree with its lights! Eventually, our Der Markt Platz manager, Will Martinell, anchored it in cement and that ended the theft.

As popular as all the decorations and activities are, the main event of the Christmas Lighting Festival is what we called "The Countdown." Every Christmas thousands of people come by train, bus and car just for this event and fill Front Street, the sidewalks and the park. As daylight fades, Christmas music is played from the bandstand and is carried by loudspeakers around the town. Then a voice is heard beginning to count—Ten...Nine...Eight...Seven. After an initial hushed reaction, the crowd joins the chant, with increasing volume. When everyone shouts One! thousands of Christmas lights are turned on all over town. Lights outline the roofs of buildings, balconies, windows, doorways, the bandstand, bell tower and trees. Each building is usually lighted in a single color that emphasizes the characteristic features of its Bavarian design. A giant fir tree in the downtown park is also covered with thousands of lights.

At the same instant the countdown ends, "Silent Night" is played from the bandstand. Throughout the town, people join hands and thousands of voices join in. Some sing the familiar "Silent Night" and some the German "Stille Nacht." From one end of town to the other there is, for that brief time, one united voice that sings of wonder—that sings a prayer of peace and love. I believe that during those few minutes in this enchanted village of light, many people feel the true sense of the Christ in their innermost being.

Art in the Park

Another highly successful Leavenworth event is Art in the Park, an outdoor art exhibition that runs from Maifest through the Autumn Leaf Festival in the downtown city park. The exhibition features a wide variety of arts, all of which are for sale. Many artists are from the Wenatchee Valley, but guest artists come from throughout the Pacific Northwest.

Art in the Park had its beginning early in 1966, evolved slowly and was plagued by difficulties, including organizational woes and financial problems. Its success is due primarily to the whole-hearted dedication of a few individuals. Indeed, that is the story of Leavenworth.

Christmas is a magical time in Leavenworth, when thousands of visitors gather to enjoy a holiday lighting tradition begun at The Squirrel Tree (this page, top right). Visits with Mr. and Mrs. Santa, sleigh rides, caroling and window shopping draw thousands to this "village of light." Bonfires blaze on Front Street to warm visitors' hands before they stop at a sidewalk vendor's stand to sample Old World foods.

Mai Fest is Leavenworth's spring festival, a weekend of traditional Bavarian dancing, singing and band music crowned by a Grand March in which everyone is invited to join. Fresh-cut flowers abound, a reminder that planting time is under way.

The Autumn Leaf Festival

features spectacular displays of fall leaves, gathered fresh from the forests and hillsides near America's Bavarian Village. This annual Indian Summer event starts on the last weekend in September and runs through the first weekend of October. The highlight of the festival is a grand parade.

For many years, I collected fresh leaves for decorating storefronts.

We started gathering leaves at Merritt Inn. Here (right) we are joined by Bob's mother in 1957.

Caramel apples, that tasty treat, represent Leavenworth's spirit of giving. In a vacant downtown building (below) volunteers help Archie and Ester Marlin make the apples. More volunteers, including Fanny and Andy Pashkowski and Liz Saunders and her children, sell the apples at festival time to support community projects. When Archie and Ester's home, the Candy Kitchen and art gallery in Tumwater Canyon burned to the ground, townspeople helped them to rebuild and furnish it.

Left. Ken Coffin's Park Haus Bulding, with cascades of flowers, is adjacent to Downtown City Park.

Art in the Park gives artists from all over the Pacific Northwest a place to showcase their work. Photographer Richard Barrington (above), who regularly exhibits in the park, has provided many of the photos in this book. When this free event began in 1966 (top right) few of the downtown buildings had become Bavarian. As the years went by, Art in Park became increasingly popular.

Art in the Park began in a modest way. When the downtown was being remodeled and most people just drove by, I remembered the outdoor art shows Bob and I had seen in California, especially in Palm Springs, and wondered why we couldn't have something like that in Leavenworth to capture the interest of passing motorists. Also, Paul Cowgill, a local artist, taught an art class in the Hart Building, and at least once took his students into the park to paint. I wondered if artists could be invited to exhibit and sell their work in the park as well as create it there.

To make all of this happen, we needed someone who could bring the artists together and plan an outdoor show. The perfect person, I thought, was Jack Dorsey, a young, well-educated and soft-spoken man from Plain, Washington, about 12 miles away. I talked to Jack and he agreed to take the lead in getting the project started. A few years ago, Jack retold the story to me in this way:

Artist June Schoenhofen and son Peter with Bob Rodgers at festival time. For many years June exhibited her fine paintings at Art in the Park.

> I know the idea started with you, Ted. You used the good ole local boy, myself, to germinate this idea with fellow people of like mind down in Leavenworth....At that time I was probably a little skeptical, to be honest about it.
>
> You drove to my dad's ranch one day...and talked with me about forming an art center in Leavenworth, so as to attract tourist interest and help promote a better cultural environment for the city, since the city was evaluating its present-future status. From there, we, a group of local artists, met with you and Bob at The Squirrel Tree Restaurant for our first art conference. I believe I officiated and discussion was free and interest high for such a move to create weekend exhibitions of local, regional and state art in the city park in Leavenworth. Next a larger group of upper valley artists met in Mrs. Hart's vacant building where Paul Cowgill was teaching oil painting.
>
> [Art In The Park] came to fruition...[and] there were these festive tents and tables and art objects and paintings—all over the park....it brought a tremendous number of people to Leavenworth.
>
> I remember seeing all types of artists and artwork down there. I remember those trees dripping sap or residue off their leaves onto my paintings! I remember the windy days, and the fun times, and just a tremendous amount of sales.....Art was in the park, and then all of a sudden you had galleries! Then you just had gallery after gallery....I've

benefitted, and other artists have benefitted for many years.

...for years this has been a good thing for Leavenworth....my children now will have the benefit to display their work at Leavenworth. My daughter has been in many, many shows. My son has had three or four national exhibitions. They both sell very well. My younger son is in college now, and hopefully we will be a family displaying in Leavenworth in the future. I am just looking forward to that day.

Mrs. Marie Conard directed the first showings—only a few paintings—on April 30 and May 1, 1966. However, a week later at the second show nearly 500 visitors came to view the paintings.

In 1966 the people who worked devotedly alongside Jack Dorsey to ensure the success of the shows were Daphne Clark, Ester and Archie Marlin, Sr., Marie Conard, Dick and Betty Baerman, Ovidia Blackburn, Bea Colvin and others.

Russ and Vera Lee promoted the shows heavily in *The Echo,* while Bob and I made the first financial contributions and ran advertisements for the shows on the local radio station. One ad was "See the Leavenworth art shows on your way to The Squirrel Tree on Saturdays and Sundays."

Late in the summer of 1966 I talked to Archie Marlin, Sr. about the further expansion of Art in the Park. I thought the shows could be expanded to five days a week and believed they definitely should become self-supporting. I also felt the merchants would be willing to help maintain the shows because, as everyone could see, they were attracting larger crowds each month.

In 1967, the crucial year for Art in the Park, Archie took over and became the first paid art director. His salary came from a 10 percent commission levied on the sales, plus donations from many of the merchants. Archie expanded the shows to five days a week and built easels for the artists, as well as a pushcart to transport the paintings. Thereafter, Archie and Ester Marlin were instrumental in making Art in the Park the successful venture it has become.

Art in the Park has not been without its problems, however. Some artists have moved into their own or cooperative galleries. Some felt the park shows presented too much competition. The city council complained about the additional maintenance costs for repairing damaged park areas. And Nature herself wasn't always a friend, for wind and rain could ruin many a work of art.

Top. In 1967, as director of Art in the Park, Archie Marlin (left) increased exhibiting time from a weekend to five days. Here Archie and Heinz Ulbricht set up a display for Art in the Park. Bottom. Woodcarvers Marianne and Ernie Bielitzer at their shop during the autumn leaf festival. Ernie built Leavenworth's first May Pole and first introduced traditional German customs for Mai Fest.

The association reorganized over the years to cope with existing problems. When it increased its commission to 20 percent of sales, profits were sufficient to maintain the park itself, to provide academic scholarships and to fund other worthwhile community activities.

Mai Fest

Spring is one of the most beautiful times of the year in the Wenatchee Valley. The hills and valleys are ablaze with daisies, trillium, lupin, mock orange and Indian paintbrush, and of course new foliage is beginning to appear everywhere. The snow is gone from the lowlands and the rivers are full, fed by melting snow from the mountains. The sweet fragrance from the cottonwood buds scents the evening air and apple and pear blossoms paint the valley pink and white. By spring, the days are warming up to very comfortable temperatures and fishermen are heading out to the streams and lakes. A light, expectant atmosphere pervades the town.

Despite all of these attributes, the early years of Leavenworth's transformation brought few visitors to town. Autumn Leaf Festival, Christmas Lighting and Art in the Park were all established by the early 1970s, but Bob and I felt a big spring event was needed. If we held a Mai Fest each year, we could offer visitors an attraction for each of the four seasons. In 1971 Bob proposed such a festival. At that time Owen Watson was chamber president, and Bob was chairman of the Merchants Committee. When his idea was finally accepted, Bob took on the duties of Mai Fest general chairman.

Because the first week of May was the time when the Washington State Apple Blossom Festival was held, we planned our festival for the second week in the month. One old timer objected to this date because it was the Sunday celebrating Mother's Day and argued that we were "commercializing on poor Mother." Yet when the first Mai Fest was held, we discovered that many visitors brought their mothers as a special treat.

Beginning with the first Mai Fest, Ernie Bielitzer took charge of the may pole, which became a focal point of the celebration. Ernie and his wife Marianne were German woodcarvers who owned and operated the Alpenhansel Shop. To make Mai Fest authentic, Ernie gathered as much information as he could from "the old country." He made and decorated many may poles and initiated the practice of using sprays of birch leaves to decorate the business district and the bandstand in the park.

"We started Art in the Park back in 1966 when there wasn't much else going on. One evening Ted Price got a group of us together who had been meeting in one of the empty store buildings on the main street. We had been having art classes there for about a year, just because we all wanted to try to paint. And so several of us met and discussed the possibility of having an art show in the park.

And out of that it grew from just a very small little art show to one that was known well all over the country, I believe. We had artists coming from just about every state in the Union and Canada. It was a great asset to the community!

— Daphne Clark

Top. For many festivals Charlie Hall was master of ceremonies at the bandstand in Downtown City Park. Bottom. Daphne Clark introduces a Swiss accordionist for an impromptu concert at the bandstand.

On Saturday, May 8, 1971, Leavenworth hosted its first Mai Fest—and what a gala occasion it was! Joy Henson, the program chairperson, brought together a variety of activities and entertainment. Reportedly, some 2,000 people attended—far more than had been expected. Many came by bus, including one busload from British Columbia.

The Washington School Edelweiss Dancers performed the traditional may pole dance, there was a Grand March led by Pauline Watson and a Mai Fest ceremony was held. Other events included Bavarian songs, a Tyrolean band, a yodeling accordianist, the Leavenworth Junior Choir and the city's newly installed carillon bells.

During the festivities, a visitor could enjoy Art in the Park or take in the flea market. There were film showings and a juried art show. Concession stands were all over the downtown area. In keeping with the theme, buckets of spring flowers were displayed outside the stores and fresh-cut balsamroot, lupin and other flowers decorated some of the store entrances. In recent years the May Pole dance, always the highlight of Mai Fest, is performed by the Enzian Dancers from Seattle.

Attending Mai Fest is a wonderful way to celebrate springtime in the Washington Cascades before large crowds have arrived in Leavenworth.

Carillon Bells

Every visitor to Leavenworth enjoys the clear, mellow ringing of the carillon bells, whose tones, sounding each hour, suffuse the whole town with a sense of peace. As Russ Lee tells it,

The carillon story is another example of community spirit. When my son Tom Lee was working in a Sun Valley ski resort, he was impressed with the sound of the Schumerich Carillons and wrote to his mother Vera that he thought they would be a logical addition to Leavenworth. In 1969 when Archie Marlin Sr. became president of the chamber, Vera passed on Tom's suggestion. With typical Marlin enthusiasm, Archie pounced upon the idea, exclaiming 'That would be the frosting on the cake!' Because of Archie's backing and perseverance the chamber approved sponsoring the carillon. Vera became chairman of the Carillon Committee. Many meetings were held determining how to finance them and choosing carillon music for a souvenir record to be sold in the shops. The carillon system was purchased on a five-year contract of $6,287. A bank loan was secured

*with $100 notes from 32 individuals. The Vesta Junior Women loaned
money, and memorials and donations were made. Joy Henson delivered
the souvenir records to the stores, and the merchants contributed all profits
to the carillon fund.*

The total contract and loans were paid off in 18 months. The first sound
of the carillon was heard throughout the community on June 20, 1969. In
1989 the carillon was replaced with a new up-to-date system which cost
$17,000. For 25 years the carillon was housed in the city hall. When that
building was sold, the new owner, Kathy Wolfe, volunteered to continue to
house the carillon system there.

Enthusiasm for the carillon continues within the community. A dream
of a traveling carillon exists, and this would cost over $200,000. Is it only
a dream?

The Marlin Handbell Ringers

When Karen Dean first heard a handbell choir, she felt it would be an
ideal performing group for Leavenworth. She brought the idea to the
roundtable at John the Baker's, where—as she put it—she raved about it for
two weeks. She first found support for the idea from Andy Pashkowski, Archie
Marlin and Mae Hamilton.

*Burning the bank mortgage
for money borrowed to buy
the carillon bells. (From left)
Vera Lee holds the bank
mortgage, Joy Henson looks
on with pleasure, Mayor
Wilbur Bon supplies the
torch and Archie Marlin
leads the townspeople's cheer.*

125

Karen researched the costs and Andy raised the money needed to purchase two octaves of handbells for $1,800. Four octaves were needed to form a choir, so Andy arranged to borrow several thousand dollars from the Carillon Committee. Archie volunteered to make and sell candy apples through his Candy Kitchen. For many years he and his helpers sold the apples at fifty cents each, and he raised over $12,000 to repay the Carillon Committee. Gradually more octaves of handbells were purchased.

Karen said that no one in town knew anything about playing a handbell, but when the first shipment of bells arrived a little pamphlet was included on "how to use the bells." That was the beginning. Karen found an excellent director for the choir in Georgette Fuller, and there was enthusiastic participation by volunteer handbell ringers from then on. The first outdoor performance of the Marlin Handbell Ringers was held on July 4, and today the choir is an established musical group in Leavenworth that has given scores of concerts over the years.

Top. Volunteer street vendors tempt visitors with caramel apples to raise money for local projects. Janet Motteler stands center and Karen Dean at the far right. Bottom. Georgette Fuller Ewing, director of the Marlin Handbell Ringers, taught piano, organ and harpsicord and arranged much of the Handbell Ringers' music. The group's name honors Archie Marlin.

Public Restrooms

As the remodeling of the town proceeded and festivals drew large crowds, the absence of any public restrooms became more and more critical. For a brief time the restrooms at city hall were open, but that proved unworkable. Nor were restaurants and service stations the answer, for owners often restricted use of their restrooms to customers, leading to loud and frequent complaints. In 1971 the parks committee I chaired studied the growing problems of restrooms and parking. Briefly, we discussed forming a local improvement district, but there was insufficient support from the business community to make this feasible. By 1977 the situation had become intolerable. To get the town moving to resolve this dilemma I contacted Daphne Clark, president of the chamber, drew up a proposal and appealed to everyone to tackle the problem the same way we had handled so many others—stop talking, stop studying and do something! I suggested that everyone donate as much money as possible and that we accept donations of cash, materials, professional skills, time and labor from any source willing to give to the project. The support we received was overwhelming. That night nine chamber members each donated $500 and others made smaller contributions.

Daphne Clark, then president of the chamber, says of that meeting: *When Ted Price said, "Let's do it. Let's go ahead with it," everybody there agreed that we should. There were contractors of various kinds, and people who had businesses here—plumbing, and electrical and building contractors. And with lots of volunteer help, and volunteer donations, the restrooms were built. I'm not sure, but with donated labor and some materials I think it was approximately $20,000 to build that first public restroom. The building turned out to be a wonderful asset to the community.*

The Marlin Handbell Ringers take a bow in an early photo, which is featured on its record album and audio tape covers.

City councilman Andy Pashkowski, a real mover and shaker, hoses the sidewalk daily in front of his and wife Fanny's shop. For several years, Andy volunteered to maintain the public restrooms free of charge.

Heinz Ulbricht donated the architectural design for the building and Emery Wechselberger volunteered his services as contractor. Owen Watson offered to do the electrical work and Dick Stroup the plumbing, while Joan James took charge of the volunteers needed for the project.

With such wonderful cooperation, everything moved forward quickly. In a short time we raised a two-story Bavarian-style building at the corner of Eighth and Commercial Street on the city-owned lot that had been used to store road equipment. The public restrooms were located on the main floor, with space for an office downstairs and an upstairs office or apartment to rent out and help pay for building maintenance. However, as soon as the restrooms were opened, long lines began forming outside and it immediately became obvious to all of us that we needed still more public facilities!

When I became president of the chamber again in 1981, I talked to Emery Wechselberger—who was planning to build Park Haus on Front Street—about a possible solution. I hoped to convince Emery to install a public restroom in the lower level of his building. Emery was one of the strongest community supporters we ever had, and he readily agreed. He added the restrooms to his building and charged the chamber only his bare expenses. Then he gave the town a 99-year lease for one dollar!

Chamber Vice President Phil Clayton took charge of raising the money needed for this project, and Chancellor Jack Koenig of the Royal Bavarians arranged for his group to contribute the balance needed to complete the job. Then one of the city councilmen, Andy Pashkowski, offered to be responsible for maintaining the restrooms, as well as the sidewalk outside. For two years Andy was out at 6:30 a.m. cleaning the restrooms and hosing down the sidewalk, always cheerful and joking and whistling as he worked. His wife Fanny said, "He'd sing in the early morning, yeah. But somebody has to do those things. That's a small part of your days, to clean the restrooms—see that they sparkle for people. That's important!"

Other volunteers, including Don May, took over when Andy was away, and again when his health deteriorated and he could no longer do the work. Later, as financial success came to Leavenworth, the city paid to have these services performed.

~ 9 ~

Leavenworth
Parks and Recreation

"Leavenworth is situated in the heart of a vast recreational area of the State of Washington. A multitude of natural recreational activities, available throughout all four seasons of the year, attract hundreds of thousands of people from the state, the Northwest and the nation....Planning for the future is vital to safeguard the environment and to preserve the natural beauty. Leavenworth's waterfront, both within the city limits and adjoining, is of paramount importance in the planning."

— *1971 Comprehensive Recreation Plan*
City of Leavenworth

The wild and beautiful Wenatchee River carves a swirling path as it courses through Leavenworth, a few hundred feet behind the downtown core of buildings. In its rambling journey through the Cascade valleys it can change from a churning white river to a serene, crystal-clear stream. As it winds through Leavenworth, it laps white sand beaches that are ideal for swimmers. Occasionally, deer, bears and beavers are seen along the river, as well as ducks, geese and other birds.

Today the splendid riverfront area of Leavenworth is available to everyone, offering a park and promenade, beaches and Blackbird Island, the jewel of the river. Visitors can choose their pleasure—walking, swimming, sunbathing, fishing, boating, kayaking, inner tubing, white water rafting, cross country skiing or communing with nature—they are all there to enjoy.

However, there was a time not too long ago when all of this was just a pipe dream, the waterfront privately owned and considered worthless. Russ Lee recalls, "When the idea came up for a waterfront park, the feeling in the city

*The 1971 Comprehensive
Recreation Plan proposed
three phases of development:
I. The core area with Blackbird Island, the promenade,
nature paths and picnic
area; II. The downstream
area with walking and bi-
cycle paths, a train and an
aerial tramway to Mountain
Home; III. The upstream
area with continuation of
the paths and train. Other:
A. Leavenworth Golf
Course; B. Tumwater Can-
yon and C. Downtown.*

council was 'another park is the last thing we need!'" Nor did everyone in town support a waterfront park system. Some wanted to bring industries to town and locate them by the water.

One proposal named Blackbird Island as the site for a possible sewer facility. Another involved building a lime reduction plant just a few hundred feet upstream from the island. In spite of denials by industrial developers, we believed that such a plant could give off a fine cement dust that would coat everything in the area, float in the air for long distances and destroy the woods and forests. The town was saved from this catastrophe by Robert B. Field, ex-banker and large property owner, who brought an injunction against the proposed plant.

1965 Leavenworth Comprehensive Recreation Plan

Early in 1965 I learned of a Washington state plan to help communities acquire and develop waterfront property for recreational purposes. Sponsored by the Washington State Inter-Agency Committee for Outdoor Recreation (generally abbreviated IAC), it gave local communities matching funds for the acquisition and development of park lands, with waterfront property given top priority. The federal government then agreed to match both city and state funds for such purchases. This meant that 25 percent of the project funding had to come from the local community, 25 percent from the state and 50 percent from the federal government. An additional benefit of IAC funding was that neither state nor federal matching funds had to be repaid.

Before Leavenworth could apply for a grant, however, we had to prepare a park and recreation plan. That was needed before we could acquire Blackbird Island, and Bob Brender and Vern Herrett agreed to help. Bob was president of the Leavenworth Chamber of Commerce, and Vern owned the Tumwater Cafe. Vern believed he could persuade Bud Christiansen, who owned the island, to sell it for $10,000. Under IAC rules, the city would only need to raise one-fourth of that amount.

To be eligible for IAC funding, however, Leavenworth needed an approved park plan and we didn't have one. In fact, Leavenworth had never had a major park plan. Many years later, as Leavenworth prospered, the city council would allocate funds to study a project, engage professionals, seek bids and arrange all the necessary interviews, surveys and conferences before a plan was written and printed. But in 1965 the city didn't have a dime to give to such a process.

Nevertheless, in May 1965 Bob Brender and I went to the city council and promised to deliver a parks and recreation plan in four months. Where the city was going to find the needed $2,500 to purchase Blackbird Island we really didn't know, but once we had a viable plan I felt sure we'd find the money somehow.

I was then chairman of the Leavenworth Chamber of Commerce Tourism Committee and, after conferring with different committee members on separate aspects of the plan, I sat down to write the document myself. We asked Mildred Roe to mimeograph the completed work, attached my own photographs and on October 28, 1965 presented it to the city council and the chamber of commerce. It was unanimously approved.

Leavenworth banker Robert B. Field was a guiding force in the town's early years. Below. This historic house on a hilltop above the Wenatchee River was built by the Lamb-Davis Lumber Company in 1903. In later years it was home to the R.B. Field family, then to Carolyn Schutte, and to Bob Rodgers and me. In 1976 Dick and Liz Saunders purchased it and with extensive renovations opened a beautiful bed and breakfast, Haus Lorelei.

In the 1965 plan the waterfront area is shown as a park, but at the time it was owned by R. B. Field. His estate was a beautiful and remarkable stretch of land extending about a half mile along a bend in the Wenatchee River downstream from Blackbird Island. The house, thought of as "the Leavenworth mansion," sits squarely on a small hill commanding a view of the river valley, the mountains and Tumwater and Icicle canyons. (Today the house is Elizabeth Saunders' Haus Lorelei, a charming bed and breakfast lodging.) In addition, the property contained Field's Bent River Arabian Horse Ranch. I always hoped that one day Field would donate this entire area to the city for everyone to enjoy.

In November Bob Brender, Bob Rodgers and I went to Olympia to present the plan to Governor Dan Evans and State Parks Director Charles Odegaard. Both endorsed it in its entirety and praised our do-it-ourselves work, especially the fact that we developed the plan without any financial support. On April 14, 1966 we finally became eligible for IAC funding.

Almost immediately the money did appear—another stroke of good fortune for Leavenworth—after we learned that Chelan County had monies for parks and recreation that had never been used Bob Brender and Vern Herrett applied to the county for these funds and on May 12 the county bought

Blackbird Island for $10,000, including IAC funding. Dick Stroup, the 1967 chamber president, worked further on this project and eventually the county simply gave the island to the town of Leavenworth.

The 1965 Comprehensive Recreation Plan proposed the following development projects, not all of which were realized:

1. Acquisition of Blackbird Island and the adjacent land
2. An extension of the golf course
3. Waterfront overnight facilities for campers and trailers
4. Improved ski facilities
5. Mountain View Point (for sightseers)
6. Great Northern Historical Park, a playground and rest area featuring the history of the Leavenworth area.

Obtaining the Land for Waterfront Park

In 1967 R. B. Field died and his riverfront home was put up for sale at $75,000. The magnificent horses were sold separately, but three horse barns remained (one of which figures in our story later on). In a bold and generous move, Carolyn Schutte bought this property in 1968, saying it was to be a gift to Bob and me.

Bob and I both felt that the waterfront land rightfully belonged to the city for everyone's enjoyment, but if we accepted Carolyn's incredibly generous offer, I thought, we could donate part of the land to the city and its appraised value could serve as Leavenworth's share for IAC funding. When I told Carolyn of my plans for creating a waterfront park, however, she questioned the idea. She preferred, she said, to give the property to Bob and me. "The people in Leavenworth do not appreciate you," she said, "but I do." After much urging, Carolyn acquiesced. "It's yours," she said finally, "to do with as you want, but I really wanted to show my appreciation for what the two of you have done here." We did not know then how seriously Carolyn's health was beginning to fail.

As it turned out, Carolyn never did transfer the property to us. In a few years Bob and I bought the house from Carolyn, along with a few surrounding acres, and we lived there happily for seven years. In August 1972 Carolyn deeded the riverfront land to the city for a waterfront park. About twice a month I would drive to Seattle and bring Carolyn to Leavenworth to stay with us for several days at her beloved Field house.

"Will the people find a way to share the valley with the deer, the beavers and the bears and other animals needing protection from human encroachment? Will people begin to realize they are not the sole inhabitants of planet earth?

Because of our profound love of animals, Bob and I have long felt that an animal refuge might be established throughout the valley over to Icicle Canyon."
— *Ted Price*

133

1968 Landscape Plan

In 1968 I was elected president of the chamber of commerce and began to turn my attention to the question of city landscaping. In those days we and other merchants were still using plastic or silk flowers as primary building decorations in our flower boxes, although Bob and I had a few hanging baskets with live flowers and other plantings.

I had close contact with Bill Talley and Mike Brooks, of the landscape architectural firm of Talley and Associates in Seattle, and wanted them to design a landscape plan that would serve Leavenworth for decades to come. I thought it essential that we have visual, long-term guidelines to coordinate plantings throughout the year. I also wanted to propose that living flowers appear everywhere in town.

Talley & Associates knew that Leavenworth was financially handicapped so they took on the project as a challenge and agreed to do it for $2,000! As usual, we didn't have $2,000 or any city funds for such professional help, but Leavenworth's benefactor, Carolyn Schutte, anonymously donated the money.

With Carolyn's donation to the city we moved ahead and the landscape plan was completed. It was an ambitious plan that emphasized developing a pedestrian-oriented town and called for visitor information facilities, shade

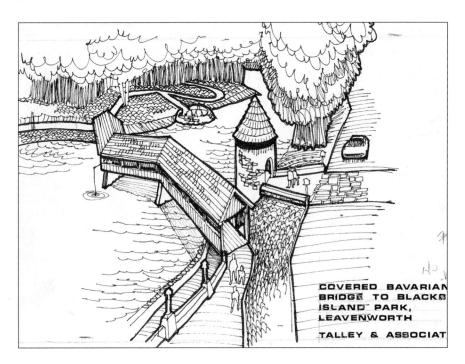

COVERED BAVARIAN
BRIDGE TO BLACK
ISLAND PARK,
LEAVENWORTH

TALLEY & ASSOCIAT

LIGHT FIXTURES

When we were in Solvang in 1965, we noted how important it was for each building to have Old World light fixtures and found a wholesale outlet for them in Fontana, California. Later, Bob and I arranged to buy the fixtures in quantity and re-sell them to building owners in Leavenworth at or near our wholesale cost. We bought enough fixtures for up to twelve buildings, which was quite a risk to take, but as we had hoped the first six buildings that were remodeled used them and by the end of 1966 other fixtures were taken up by additional building owners.

Below. Walt Rembold, a former high school teacher and a photographer, delivers flowers to Der Markt Platz for spring planting. Walt and his wife Vi were active volunteers in Leavenworth's revitalization. Many of Walt's photographs, taken from the 1960s to the early 1980s, are reproduced in this book.

tree planting, off-street parking, a profusion of live flowers, a Bavarian-style fountain, distinctive street lights, a riverfront trail system and a covered bridge to Blackbird Island (a smaller version of the one we'd photographed in Lucerne, Switzerland). Regarding future commercial developments, the plan suggested that the key to architectural design was an informal arrangement of buildings and spaces.

Unfortunately, we were unable to carry out the 1968 plan. We simply didn't have the resources—the money, leadership, staff and volunteer help—to stay with the program year after year. But the seeds (perhaps an apt metaphor) had been planted, and today some of the goals of the 1968 plan have been met. One way we achieved them was through a new comprehensive recreation plan, adopted in 1971.

Flowers, Flowers, Flowers !

Throughout our early years in Leavenworth, one of the greatest wishes Bob and I shared was to see the town overflowing with live flowers. Although they require steady maintenance, they are one of the least expensive ways to beautify an area, be it a home, business, street or entire town. Remembering our experience at The Squirrel Tree, and the help we had received from Tiny, we tried to introduce more and more flowers into Leavenworth and encourage other building owners to install lots of flower boxes, hanging baskets and sidewalk planters. However, in the early days

Above. Karen Dean and her mother Virginia contributed greatly to developing Leavenworth's cultural affairs and to the widespread use of fresh flowers. Here Karen and Virginia are planting flowers in time for Mai Fest.

Opposite. Leavenworth shops and homes are adorned with blossoms and greenery from early spring through late autumn. Old-style street lamps, once removed by the city and stored, now grace Front Street.

of the town's revival we were poor as church mice and felt that maintenance of live flowers would be a major problem, so we settled for artificial flowers.

In the early 1970s the cause of live flowers was revived when Karen Dean arrived on the scene—another case of the right person appearing at precisely the right time. Karen considers herself a purist, and when she saw all our artificial flowers "blooming" at zero degrees with waist-high snow on the ground, I guess she thought, "These have to go!" Karen launched an ambitious project not only to replace the artificial flowers but to expand the use of live flowers throughout the village. She bought flats and flats of various flowers, transported them into town and sold them to merchants at cost. She also joined forces with Ernie Bielitzer, who wanted to plant edelweiss, the state flower of Bavaria, throughout the mountains near Leavenworth. The profusion of flowers you see in the village today is mainly the work and inspiration of Karen Dean.

Karen, Charles Pearson, Bob Rodgers and I bought whiskey barrels, cut them in half, and made outdoor planters that were placed on sidewalks.

About 1970 Bob and I had started using large flower baskets from Saxe Floral in Seattle, and later we did everything we could to encourage merchants to buy big hanging baskets, offering to handle orders, pick up and delivery. We brought the baskets into town in quantity, some pre-sold at cost to merchants who wanted them, others as gifts for new businesses. At first I'd simply load up our car with the number of flower baskets we needed, but during part of the 1970s Bob and I paid Walt Rembold to truck the flower baskets in from Seattle.

Bob and I had flower barrels filled with petunias and geraniums positioned along two sides of Der Markt Platz. When we remodeled, we added many hanging baskets, installed flower boxes on the balconies that ran along two sides of the building and placed more barrels of flowers on the sidewalks—in part to show other building owners how flowers could transform a building into a showcase for the town. In the mid- to late 1970s Chuck Langlois and Andy Pashkowski proposed that merchants hire a high school student to care for the live flowers daily and wash down the sidewalks.

About 1980 newcomer Don May, volunteered to help with decorations for the Christmas Lighting Festival. He soon proved to be very knowledge-

Alpine Scenes surround Leavenworth, offering tranquility and a variety of recreational opportunities. The wild Wenatchee River attracts rafters, while Watefront Park and Blackbird Island are great spots for quiet walks, swimming and sunbathing. In spring and summer, hillsides are covered with flowers and the area abounds with wildlife. Recently, bird watching has become popular.

able about flower maintenance, so Bob and I hired him to take care of our flowers and Der Markt Platz sidewalks. Soon Don was hired by other building owners, and within a few years he opened his own business called A Bavarian Caretaker.

I've never thought Don's contribution to the town has been fully acknowledged. He had a natural ability with flowers and always took great pride in his work. During the hot summer he would begin making his rounds to care for the flowers in the wee hours of the morning. His concern for Leavenworth was such that he even tended the flowers of merchants who hadn't actually hired him to do so.

When Bob and I purchased hanging baskets for the bandstand and flower barrels to be installed downtown, we had our shop employees water them for a few years, but later Don May cared for them at no charge to the city. Before Bob and I sold Der Markt Platz in 1986, we were happy that Art in the Park, under the direction of Will Martinell, took on this responsibility, as well as responsibility for maintaining the park in general. To help with the park maintenance, we gave the city our riding lawn mower. Will's daughter Lisa, continues to care for the lawn and flowers in the downtown park.

Both Karen Dean and Don May deserve a great deal of credit—and gratitude—for developing the rich live floral displays now seen everywhere in Leavenworth. Their work has inspired many other towns throughout the Northwest to decorate their streets and buildings in a similar fashion.

1971 Comprehensive Recreation Plan

Owen Watson was president of the chamber of commerce when I proposed we create a parks and recreation committee and volunteered to draw up a revised recreation plan. Owen and the chamber wholeheartedly agreed.

With Carolyn Schutte's permission and at my own expense, I engaged Creative Engineering of Wenatchee to survey her property. We divided the estate into three parcels and provided legal descriptions of each: (1) all of the riverfront strip that was to become the new Waterfront Park; (2) a parcel of land, part of which was to be for city use and part a charitable trust where someday a castle and other Bavarian-style buildings, cultural facilities and a parking area would rise; (3) the house and grounds of the old Field home, where Bob and I would live.

Above. Lisa (Martinell) McGee regularly maintains the flowers adorning the bandstand and Downtown City Park.

Opposite. The beautiful Wenatchee River can be a raging white-water torrent or a crystal clear stream as it winds through the Leavenworth valley.

Page 138, top right. Renee Johnson picking balsamroot.

Page 139, clockwise from top left. Scenes along the Wenatchee River include Blackbird Island, the dam in Tumwater Canyon, rafters, and (below) Donna (Rembold) Brunz and her children greeting kayakers at Waterfront Park.

The waterfront promenade in a Swiss village, one of the many photographs I took in Europe that inspired my recommendations for the 1971 park plan and the designs for Leavenworth's Waterfront Park.

Late in 1969 Bob and I returned to Europe to photograph waterfront promenades. We intended to use the photos in designing the Leavenworth riverfront areas. Additionally, we collected brochures and photographs of some European cities with waterfront areas. But it was in Lugano and Lucarno, Switzerland, on the Italian border, that we found the ideas and designs we liked best.

Because of its fantastic mountain and river views, we envisioned this strip of riverfront as a "passive" park—one with a promenade and wide waterfront trails meant for sitting, walking, enjoying the magnificent landscape and bird watching. Others in town preferred an "active" park with swings and slides, ballparks and sports facilities for children and adults. There also were those who didn't want a park at all, for they felt it would attract riffraff, "hippies" and other undesirable outsiders. Still others seemed to feel that Leavenworth was simply changing too fast, and for a few resentment of me seemed to be a factor.

In the revised plan, I used photographs from Switzerland to introduce several new ideas, including an Old European-style promenade with sidewalk cafes and shops, street lamps, fountains and possibly statuary. We suggested installing a narrow-gauge railway to run locally through a small portion of the scenic Leavenworth valley. In addition to expanding the cross-country ski trails, we urged the development of mountain sports such as skiing and sleigh-

Leavenworth's European-style promenade in Waterfront Park adjacent to downtown. Locals have dubbed this lovely park "the Vienna Woods." The banks of the Wenatchee lie a few feet to the right.

ing. We considered a lift or tramway to Mountain Home, as well as alpine lifts to new ski areas. Our recommendations for environmental harmony included maintaining an open waterfront with a green belt on both sides of the Wenatchee River, wildlife protection and building and sign regulations.

We completed the revised plan ourselves, without professional assistance, and in December 1971 it was presented to the chamber, the city council and the IAC. It was enthusiastically accepted by Leavenworth officials, but the IAC thought the appraised figure of $150,000 for Waterfront Park property was too high to match with $450,000 in IAC funding.

I wanted an additional park entry from 9th Street, a roadway leading to off-street parking and one that would serve the remaining property owned by Carolyn Schutte. Had Carolyn been in good health, I would have hired an engineer to prepare a legal description for a roadway. However, this would be time consuming, and daily we risked losing funding for the park.

With Carolyn's approval, I solved the problem quite simply. With a pen and ruler I squared out enough land for an entry to the park, an improvement that would bring the appraisal up to the needed $150,000. This alteration was acceptable at the time, but little did we realize that this road would not become a city street and the property would be left without adequate legal access. By May 1972 funding for the new section of park downstream from Blackbird Island had been completed for $600,000, with $150,000 coming

The Leavenworth Fish Hatchery is located about five miles from town on Icicle Creek. It was once the world's largest salmon hatchery, but in 1995 only a bare trickle of some 461 salmon returned, perhaps the lowest in hatchery history.

from the appraised value of Carolyn Schutte's gift of the Waterfront Park property. This donation, along with the newly revised park plans, had made Leavenworth eligible for $450,000 in IAC funding.

In 1972 Wolf Bauer, a hydraulics engineer from Seattle, notified the park board that the channel around Blackbird Island was silting in. Bauer was then asked to draw up alternative plans for developing the park, but in the end the city decided to follow the original promenade scheme.

The winning bid for the overall park layout and landscaping came from Talley and Associates, a Seattle-based firm. Rod Simpson, one of Leavenworth's two architects, won the contract to design new restrooms, a mini open-air outdoor stage and other features. Creative Engineering, of Wenatchee, was also retained.

Russ Lee, still a vigorous supporter of a revitalized Leavenworth, became mayor in January 1972. In June of that year the city council established Waterfront Park Board and I was appointed its chairman. Russ Lee and I at-

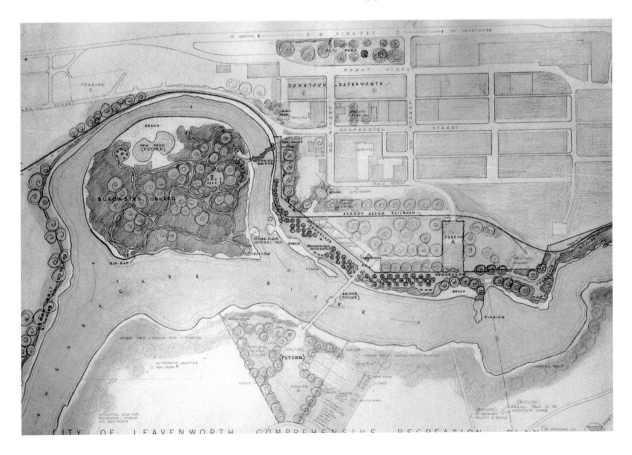

tended meetings in other towns at my expense, including IAC meetings in Olympia and meetings with the state ecology department.

With the additional IAC funds, we hoped to carry out all of the park design features, including a beautiful covered footbridge to Blackbird Island which Talley and Associates redesigned from our photographs and sketches. Unfortunately, no one was able to build the covered bridge within the budget, and a plain, very sturdy walking bridge was erected instead. When a walkway ramp was needed from the bridge to Blackbird Island, park-development money was already exhausted, but Emery Wechselberger, with his sons Eric and Roy and other volunteers, pitched in and built one. Without fanfare, they went quietly to the island in the wee morning hours and soon had completed their work.

Another of the continuing problems with the waterfront area was, and is, flooding in the spring and at other flood times, when runoffs from melting snow occasionally inundate portions of Blackbird Island, the promenade, the trails and the parking lot.

When working on the 1971 park plan, I realized that the land across the Wenatchee should be tied into the park as well. This was an area of perhaps five acres, with some 600 feet of waterfront. Bob and I signed an earnest money option to purchase this property for $8,000. To qualify for IAC funds the city would have to pay $2,000 as its share. Again, where was this initial payment to come from? LaVerne Peterson formed a committee and in the

One of the main objections to creating Waterfront Park was that there were absolutely no city funds to maintain it. In the beginning, volunteers acted as caretakers.

summer of 1972 held an auction in the Downtown City Park, a very successful event that produced the needed amount, which she gave to the city to buy the land across the river in East Leavenworth.

At this time Russ Lee resigned as mayor and Councilman Chuck Bowen was named to fill the office temporarily. When an election was called to name a mayor for the remainder of Lee's term, I decided to run. The truth is that I absolutely dreaded entering the mayoral race, but I could see no other way to sustain the momentum we'd achieved in Leavenworth.

But this wasn't to be. In a very close race—less than 40 votes— Chuck Bowen was elected mayor. Under the new administration I found it hard to work as freely as I had in the past. In deciding what I should do, I realized that I didn't want to become a source of contention, nor did I want to be involved in a personality conflict. So once more I chose to withdraw, to step down from the posts I held then—chairman of the Waterfront Park Board, vice-chairman of the Leavenworth Planning Commission and other offices, official and unofficial. I was under much stress and felt the need to back off from some of my Leavenworth work.

The Legacy of Carolyn Schutte

In the midst of our efforts to create Waterfront Park, Carolyn Schutte's health completely deteriorated. She found it hard to manage her own affairs, and it was evident that soon she would not be able to make her own decisions. When Carolyn suffered what appeared to be a series of strokes, she was taken to a special Christian Science recovery facility near Portland, where she remained for about a year.

In August 1973 Chuck Langlois, president of the chamber, had a potluck to honor Carolyn for her contributions to Leavenworth. I wanted us to honor Carolyn's many gifts to the town and its people with a bronze plaque, and I thought it appropriate to install the plaque at a principal viewpoint in Waterfront Park. Harry Butcher of nearby Cashmere helped compose our tribute. The engraved plaque speaks of Carolyn's deep commitment to serve God by helping people and animals. I took it to her bedside, and although her faculties were very weak and she was no longer able to speak, she managed to smile her approval. I know that she was pleased. A mere plaque, regardless of how highly its words praised her is, of course, not adequate recognition for everything that Carolyn did so that Leavenworth might be what it is today.

Carolyn's longtime nurse knew of our close friendship, and one day in December 1973 she phoned me in Leavenworth to say she felt Carolyn's passing was imminent. She said that Carolyn had always responded well to me and that perhaps I should come to her now. I drove straight down to Portland, but when I arrived Carolyn was no longer conscious. As I sat near her, a very light feeling went through me, like a presence, and I knew she was passing.

Carolyn died having never seen the completed Waterfront Park, a beautiful legacy she made possible for generations of residents and visitors to enjoy.

Another dream was fulfilled when Carolyn Schutte signed the deed transferring riverfront property to the city of Leavenworth—and thus insured the establishment of Waterfront Park. From left: Mayor Russ Lee, me, Carolyn, Elsa Bradford (Carolyn's sister), and notary Harry Butcher. Harry's dedication and work helped make Waterfront Park a reality.

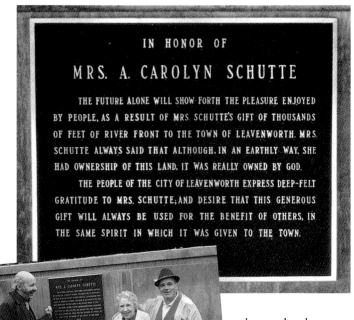

IN HONOR OF

MRS. A. CAROLYN SCHUTTE

THE FUTURE ALONE WILL SHOW FORTH THE PLEASURE ENJOYED
BY PEOPLE, AS A RESULT OF MRS. SCHUTTE'S GIFT OF THOUSANDS
OF FEET OF RIVER FRONT TO THE TOWN OF LEAVENWORTH. MRS.
SCHUTTE ALWAYS SAID THAT ALTHOUGH, IN AN EARTHLY WAY, SHE
HAD OWNERSHIP OF THIS LAND, IT WAS REALLY OWNED BY GOD.

THE PEOPLE OF THE CITY OF LEAVENWORTH EXPRESS DEEP-FELT
GRATITUDE TO MRS. SCHUTTE; AND DESIRE THAT THIS GENEROUS
GIFT WILL ALWAYS BE USED FOR THE BENEFIT OF OTHERS, IN
THE SAME SPIRIT IN WHICH IT WAS GIVEN TO THE TOWN.

A bronze plaque honoring Carolyn Schutte is installed on a viewing platform in Waterfront Park. In writing this tribute, Harry Butcher and I were inspired by Ralph Waldo Trine's "In Tune With the Infinite." Below. At the dedication of Waterfront Park (from left) is the landscape architect Bill Talley, Carolyn's sister Elsa Bradford, and Leavenworth architect Rod Simpson.

This remarkable woman gave Leavenworth so very much: she donated the half-mile stretch of Wenatchee River land, then valued at over $150,000, that made Waterfront Park possible; she contributed $1,100 to kick off the drive to build a much-needed bandstand in the Downtown City Park; she paid the entire cost of the 1968 Leavenworth Comprehensive Landscape Plan and she made it possible in very particular ways for Bob and me to move forward with many of our ideas for Bavarian Leavenworth. One can only wonder about her many other charitable acts for other people in other places, most of which I'm sure were anonymous. Carolyn was always very clear about why she came to Leavenworth: she knew she was brought here, not only for us, but for everyone. It was as though she knew she had a spiritual mission, and she fulfilled it beautifully.

A European-style park along the Wenatchee River became a reality in July 1973 and Waterfront Park was formally dedicated on October 5, 1976, in a ceremony at which Mayor Chuck Bowen officiated. Fittingly, Carolyn Schutte's sister, and my good friend, Mrs. Elsa Bradford, came to Leavenworth and spoke at the dedication. Disappointingly, my work in creating Waterfront Park was not even acknowledged.

Further Park Developments

The last phase of the 1971 plan included the entire waterfront area from Blackbird Island upstream to the Leavenworth golf course. In the mid-1970s the city acquired this property, primarily to extract sand and gravel to repave the city streets, leaving the land itself available as park land.

Carolyn Schutte's cousin Bob Weinhagen had inherited most of her estate, including her Leavenworth property. About 1975 I purchased this property from him at its taxable appraised valuation of $35,000. Not only would the property provide more land for the park trail system, Bob and I wanted to use part of it to establish a charitable trust. We intended to use the trust funds for cultural activities, solutions to the parking problem and assistance for those

"THAT BARN"—A PROJECT FOR HIGH SCHOOL STUDENTS

From our earliest days in Leavenworth we were told that young people felt left out—and some times resentful—of community efforts to develop tourism, so early in the summer of 1976 Bob and I created a project designed to bring young people into the business life of the community. We wanted to create a practical, ongoing training program for the students, as well as expose them to community involvement. It would help young people understand the economic role of tourism in revitalizing their town. Our schoolhouse was to be one of three barns Bob and I owned on the former Field estate near Waterfront Park, which we called "That Barn."

That Barn was to be a retail gift shop operated entirely by high school students. The project was approved by the school, and Bob and I worked to guide the operations. A few contributors joined in and loaned enough money to buy merchandise, while Bob and I paid for other expenses, including building an access roadway to That Barn from 9th Street in downtown Leavenworth. Artist Cordi Chamberlin Bradburn donated her time to paint Bavarian-theme murals on one of the barns, and we bought living flowers with which the students decorated That Barn.

First, the students had to get the barn in a clean, usable condition. They removed the Arabian horse stalls, painted the building and prepared it for customers. The students themselves voted not to receive a salary. Miles and Jane Turnbull, publishers of *The Echo*, reported: "The pay was rotten: nothing an hour, with nothing-and-a-half for overtime!"

Bob and I took three students on a buying trip to the Portland Gift Show to demonstrate how to select inexpensive merchandise. The students also planned to sell items made in the school shop. In the short time That Barn was open for business, few tourists wandered from the Bavarian downtown area and found their way to the shop, sales were poor and the students lost interest. There wasn't enough money to pay them even if they had voted themselves salaries. Unfortunately, by mid-summer That Barn closed. Walt and Vi Rembold offered to store the unsold merchandise in their garage for a couple of years, or until renewed interest might appear. When there was

none, Bob and I refunded the money to the original backers, then sold the merchandise at Der Markt Platz to recover at least some of our expenses.

Former mayor Will Martinell led the movement to complete Leavenworth's park system, including a second bridge from Blackbird Island upstream to the newly established Enchantment Park. Working closely with the Leavenworth Winter Sports Club and other groups, Will helped develop miles of cross-country ski trails which today enable thousands of outdoor enthusiasts to enjoy the spectacular mountain, forest and river scenery surrounding Leavenworth.

who work to help destitute people and who provide for animal welfare.

In 1981 Heinz Ulbricht and I worked on a plan for a Bavarian-style resort hotel adjoining the park. The plan was presented to the chamber and enthusiastically accepted. I also worked quietly on ideas for other projects unrelated to the park, including a much-needed underground parking garage, a performing arts center, and a new city hall, to be built adjacent to the downtown core area on Carolyn Schutte's property.

Finally, one of my impossible dreams was a Leavenworth castle along the river, perhaps a smaller version of the famous Neuschwanstein castle in Bavaria. I asked Heinz Ulbricht to design such a castle—one that was to be far more than a tourist attraction. The castle Heinz designed included a hotel, restaurant, shops and a theater, with underground parking for hundreds of cars nearby.

About 1987, when Will Martinell, former city councilman, became mayor, his top priority was the next phase of park development—extension of Waterfront Park to provide an area for cross-country skiing. Will realized that Leavenworth was in bad need of something to boost its economy in the wintertime and drew on the 1971 plan to develop a trail system for walking, cross-country skiing and related uses.

To complete the trails from downtown Leavenworth to the golf course, the city needed additional property bordering Waterfront Park and possibly an area extending back around Blackbird Island. Bob and I owned much of this land and gave what was needed to the city. When the adjoining property around Blackbird Island proved to be unavailable, another route for a pathway had to be devised. Mayor Martinell and the city decided to build a second bridge from Blackbird Island to the upstream park area, bypassing the unavailable land.

Bob and I also gave three small parcels of nearby waterfront property for use as a viewpoint and as park access from the eastern end of town. In the early 1980s the land was conservatively appraised at $20,000, making our land gift eligible for IAC funding.

In spite of opposition, the city received Blackbird Island and Waterfront Park without paying for any part of it. (This is the first time this information has been made public.) Now all of the waterfront downstream and upstream from Blackbird Island is accessible for public use and one of my dreams has truly been realized.

STREET LAMPS

In the late 1950s, before the idea of Bavarian Leavenworth had been discussed, the city council had decided to upgrade the street lighting and remove the "old-fashioned" street lamps that for many years had lined the downtown streets. Unfortunately, these relatively attractive lamps were replaced with glaringly ugly modern fixtures. By 1966, with remodeling in full swing, many of us wished we had the old street lamps back again, for they were much more in keeping with the Old World atmosphere we were trying to create.

In the mid-1970s the streets and sidewalks had to be completely rebuilt and the sidewalks widened to accommodate the increasing crowds coming to town. By now the city council was becoming more favorable to tourism and the Alpine theme, and its members agreed to leave adequate space along the new sidewalks so that the old street lamps could be easily installed. (Heinz Ulbricht made sure that the street designs included provisions for a proper wiring system.)

For several years no one knew where the old street lamps were, but then Heinz, with the help of former building inspector Bill Stevens, located them. Many had been damaged, so Bob and I offered more secure space in one of our barns. There they remained until about 1980, when they were moved to the city hall basement. Dick and Liz Saunders had since acquired the Tannenbaum Building, and at their own expense they installed street lamps there.

About 1984, when we wanted to reinstall the old street lamps, Heinz made the following offer: with some help, and the donation of adequate funds for replacement parts, he would restore the old lamps. Heinz also proposed adding a large arm near the top of each post so that two big flower baskets could hang from either side. His fee would be $500 per street lamp, without flowers, which was very low and probably gave Heinz no profit.

Bob and I felt it important to re-install these old lamps downtown, so we paid Heinz to place six of them along two blocks of Front Street, from the Edelweiss Hotel up to the Tannenbaum Building. We then purchased two large flower baskets for each one. Art in the Park Association paid for the work on three more for the park side of Front Street, and other building owners paid for three more. As his contribution to the project for a few years, "Bavarian Caretaker" Don May tended the flowers on all of them at no charge.

1994 Downtown City Park Renovations

The oldest park in Leavenworth is the one located across Front Street from the core of downtown Bavarian buildings. Over the years this park has been kept groomed and landscaped by several women's organizations, including garden clubs and the Vesta Junior Women's Club and maintained by the City of Leavenworth.

In the early 1990s Mayor Will Martinell, assisted by City Manager Mike Cecka, led the way to regrooming the entire park to make it a showplace the whole town could be proud of. Surveys and plans were begun and when Mel Wyles succeeded Will as mayor, he saw to it that all of these plans were carried out: the park was completely remodeled, the bandstand moved, a state-of-the-art sound system installed, "new" Old European-style light fixtures purchased, new restrooms built and brick paths installed. All of this was accomplished for around $850,000, and now the downtown park is more beautiful than ever.

Above. An ornate European street lamp installed in the newly re-landscaped Downtown City Park. Right. The new City Hall and Library, completed in 1995 across from Downtown City Park. LaVerne Peterson, an early pioneer in Leavenworth's revitalization, continued to be an outstanding supporter of citizen involvement. With her is her son, Mayor Mel Wyles. Mel and City Manager Mike Cecka completed the redevelopment of Downtown City Park.

~ 10 ~

The Future of Leavenworth

*"The future's still wide open. We don't know how or what [will happen].
But we are involved and committed to that future, and to see to it...that
it's as healthy in a holistic sense as we can help to make it.... I think
health and growth comes...from diversity. We grow when people are
challenging us with their diversity. If we all gather with like-minded
folk, we're in agreement to begin with. There's no challenge. There's no
growth. And so diversity is not simply an option or something to put up
with—it's essential.*

— Reverend Carl Florea

Bob and I no longer live in Leavenworth. We have sold all of the businesses
and most of the property we owned. But I return frequently, and of course
I continue to have dreams and ideas for Leavenworth's future.

The Great Fire of 1994

In 1994 a raging fire threatened that future. A lightning storm ignited
catastrophic wildfires that swept across 180,000 forested acres in Chelan County
and came within a few feet of downtown Leavenworth. Mayor Mel Wyles
vividly describes what happened:

*Now the fire that happened in the summer of 1994 was something that
Leavenworth was not even ready for....[The people of] Leavenworth
couldn't even in their wildest dreams ever conceive what happened!*

*It first started up Tumwater Canyon, and that was a lightning-strike
fire. They were fighting it the best way they could, but it kept coming
towards Leavenworth. Well, within a few days after that, a man-made
fire, by accident, was started in what they call the Rat Creek area which*

is Icicle Canyon. My water plant operator came to my house and said, "Mel, it's going to destroy the water plant!" At that time we had chlorine bottles up there, four of them, at 200 pounds-a-piece. He felt if they had exploded, they'd be just like bombs! I mean, if they landed in the middle of Leavenworth, it's hard to say what it would have done to the town.

Mayor Mel Wyles

So he and I went up there. With the assistance of the PUD and the firefighters up there at the time, we shut the water plant down and took the chlorine bottles and were loading them. But at that time I stopped, and I heard this howling noise, a screeching. It was like a wild animal! And the wind was blowing so hard! And with the noise and everything, and the fire...I'd never heard anything like it in my life!

They said, hey, it's time to go!—we can't stop it! By the time we had travelled approximately four miles it completely blew up! And it was just a towering inferno—kind of like that movie....And when it roared out of the mouth of that canyon, it scared everybody so bad! Leavenworth was put on what they call a Number One Alert.

It came down to approximately five minutes of evacuating the whole city of Leavenworth! They had firefighting equipment behind each and every home, foaming them if they had to. These people were working day and night.

I went the next morning to the flight aviation's officer for the whole fire. I said, "Dale, I don't know how to tell you this, but we need a miracle! You've got to save Icicle Ridge and the Tumwater Mountain!" So they brought in an extra aircraft specially built to drop retardant. They had twelve regular aircraft, helicopters, they were flying.

We had firefighters here from 24 different states, from Florida to Alaska. And through the help of the DNR [Department of Natural Resources], and the Forest Service, and the National Guard, and the DOT [Department of Transportation], and the Sheriff's Department—it was through all their help, all their caring, is the only way Leavenworth is here today. Other than that, we'd [have] lost it. It was that tough of a situation, that dangerous of a situation.

I mean, there were cinders falling all over around my house here in town. When you look it right straight in the face, and it isn't a mile away...! I mean, I've been in war and everything, but...I can only tell you how scared these folks were.

Hundreds of men and women from the National Guard arrive to combat the blaze, while Marines from Camp Pendleton in California battle it on the far side of the mountain. Day and night, retardant chemicals and water were dropped from helicopters in an aerial bombardment.

We had the best firefighters in the world come out of Arizona. And what's really strange is that you saw little towns like Tillamook, Oregon and Rockaway, Oregon—small towns, sending everything that they had with their volunteers. These folks, a lot of them, never received full pay, like in their normal jobs. So they accepted the fact that they were going to take a possible financial loss, to do what they believed in. Which was to save Leavenworth, the people's homes, and the people themselves. You cannot ask anymore of a human being than to do that! They were willing to give their lives!

A year later there were countless blackened trees and scarred landscapes, but new growth is visible everywhere...and it is still among the most beautiful places in the world!

Around the turn of the century, fires destroyed downtown Leavenworth, and now, again, the great fire of 1994 served as a dramatic reminder of how temporary all material existence is. We saw how quickly Bavarian Leavenworth could have disappeared, leaving only rubble and sorrow. And then, once again,

"Wedge Mountain burned in approximately twenty minutes, with flames reaching as much as two to three hundred feet. A smoke and ash cloud rose about 16,000 feet in height, and that cloud [of burning cinders] dumped on the town. At night you could see the ring of fire all around you, and of course the ash [was] dropping on you, and on your homes, and in the trees and around your property. We put sprinklers on the roof of the house periodically to keep the roof wet. We sprayed trees with waterhoses. Downtown was shut off to cars...you [had to] walk. Firetrucks, fires hoses [were] everywhere. For about three days, the smoke and ash were so thick it was very unhealthy. People became melancholy and depressed, with the smoke and the fire, and wondered what was going to happen."

— *Richard Barrington*

Reported in a special edition of *The Leavenworth Echo*, "Fires of '94"—

Fatalities: None	Bulldozers: 54
Homes Destroyed: 19	Helicopters: 12
Firefighters (from many states): 2486	Retardant dropped: 527,000 gallons
Fire engines: 268	Water dropped: 3,768,000 gallons
Fire tenders: 62	

In the summer of 1994 Leavenworth was like a war zone. When the fires threatening Leavenworth were under control, when firefighters, military personnel and scores of other volunteers were leaving and then when local, state and federal leaders sought disaster relief funds for the town, these words appeared in *The Leavenworth Echo*:

"In considering our future, it's instructive to remember our past. Self-help has been elemental to the Leavenworth success story. Its transformation from a shuttered, half-empty logging town into a vibrant destination for visitors has been accomplished with private financing. People with a commitment to Leavenworth and a belief in its future dug into their own pockets to turn their dream into reality.

"So it must be now. If we are going to recover from the fires—and we will—we are going to have to make it happen. Outside help will be much appreciated and, ultimately, will be necessary, because it's out-of-towners who provide livelihoods for the bulk of businesses in town.

"But it's also important to keep in mind that Leavenworth doesn't need patronage because it's a charity case. Tourists needn't visit out of sympathy. They can, should and will come to verify for themselves that the warmth of its inhabitants matches that which seared its borders just a few days ago."

— Jim Davis, Publisher
The Leavenworth Echo, August 10, 1994

the people of Leavenworth would have had to raise a new town from the ashes.

The Spirit of Leavenworth— A Challenge and an Opportunity

Leavenworth's history proves that it could become a "village of light," not only at Christmastime but throughout the year. In facing challenges and problems as they have, the people of Leavenworth have also had—and continue to have—the opportunity to inspire other towns throughout the country by developing pilot-project solutions to nearly universal problems.

One thing seems certain: even with fires, floods and other natural catastrophes, the future of Leavenworth is entirely dependent on the attitude of the people. As Bavarian Leavenworth came into national recognition, Alfred E. Driscoll, president of the National Municipal League, said, "The concern and involvement of ordinary citizens is our best—perhaps our only—hope of solving the serious crises facing our cities today."

In his current book, *Revolution of the Heart*, Bill Shore presents the experiences of many who, like himself, left politics to do good works. They discovered that every social and economic problem could be met with citizen involvement—what Shore calls "voluntarism." Shore states that indeed a revolution is essential and that it has to come from the heart. Government programs and funding are not enough, nor is private charity. Leavenworth has demonstrated Shore's contention admirably.

It is impossible to overemphasize the importance of active community involvement by the townspeople, merchants and building owners. The incredible volunteer efforts of everyone over the years are what transformed all our impossible dreams and foolish ideas into reality. As Bavarian Leavenworth struggled into existence, the business community was small enough so that at our regular meetings there could be brainstorming sessions, disagreements—even in-fighting—and still the ideas flowed and good solutions to problems were found. A strong central core was formed among us.

One of the most significant effects of the town's rebirth was that Leavenworth became, in Karen Dean's words, "one of the few places where women could be in business." Women have enjoyed a genuine equality with men, and they have assumed creative leadership roles.

Meetings, meetings, meetings—crucial to citizen involvement. Here the Chamber of Commerce meets in the late 1960s to approve final designs for new Bavarian-style roadway signs marking the approaches to Leavenworth. Each member is also head of a committee. Left to right are Ted Taylor, Dick Baerman, Bob Rodgers, Rena Stroup, Dee Taylor, me, Hazel Hansen, LaVerne Peterson, Ester and Archie Marlin and Cliff Hedeen (artist presenting designs).

Community Spirit.

Along with dedicated longtime residents, many creative and talented people have been drawn to Leavenworth over the years.

This page, clockwise. Royal Lady Rena Stroup; Marge and Harry Butcher with Bob Rodgers; Linda Marks; Walt Rembold; Bill Hansen; Christa Ulbricht; Nile Saunders; Lee West; Liz and Jeff Gauger, current publishers of The Echo; *Thomas L. Green, Jr.; and Chet Endrizzi.*

Opposite page, clockwise. Beth Warman; (from left) Bob Rodgers, Carl and Jenny Evans, Joe and Jan Delvo and me; Karen Dean with Archie Marlin (left) and Andy Pashkowski; Carolyn Schutte with her dog Wendy; Mai Fest marchers (from left) Bertha and Lenard Smith, Marion Speer, Heinz Ulbricht, Hazel Hansen, Mayor Wilbur and Alverda Bon, Bob Rodgers and Pauline Watson (facing away); Pat and Ed Rutledge, Sheriff Mike Brickert; Rev. Carl Florea; and (center, left to right) Charlie Hall, Miles Turnbull and Owen Watson.

Clockwise, from top left. Bill and Diane Wells; Eleanor Culling, 1996 Royal Lady and founder and conductor of the Village Voices; Emery Wechselberger; Vern Peterson; Ken Marson (left) with his parents Marydell and Gordon Marson; Leavenworth's Little Bavarian Band playing only for fun; me with Tim Easterly and Harry Butcher; and Peter Schoenhofen.

How in the world could a community this size accomplish what it did—[that] would be a textbook in itself. If you're in business, [and] you're part of this community, time and financial support are ongoing issues. There's never an end in sight, because Leavenworth is a breathing, living entity. And if we aren't growing, we're stagnating. If you stagnate, you start to die.

The dream that built this community will never die. And the Chamber as a good parent has to tug and push and pamper and encourage people to keep fixed on that dream.

It's just like any family, there'll be some bickering internally amongst children, you know, [but] there's always the responsibility of people in the position of parent, as a leader, [to] give the time and the effort to guide people through crises and keep people motivated.

The renewal of commitment is essential—the spirit, catching the vision, the continuous renewing. The patience—trying to guide people that we're all in this together and let's make this the very best community and destination in the world...that's an ongoing task, and we have a lot of talented, dedicated people here.

There again, it's the sacrifice. The sacrifice of digging deep into your pockets, not just once in a while, but time after time after time again...But that's exactly the vision and the commitment that built the village in the first place! Those things just don't go away—there's an ongoing commitment. If you want better schools, if you want good fire protection, if you want a good hospital clinic, the commitment is deep pockets—you must dig and dig again.

Beyond that, you must take the time to serve in your community...And I would be very frank about the hours and hours and hours of meetings, and [of serving on] committees—it's that type of commitment. If they don't have that type of commitment, whatever their endeavors, they are not going to succeed. So [we] just get a little brutal on just how tough it was to round up everybody to attend meeting after meeting.

Laura Jobin
Executive Director,
Leavenworth Chamber of Commerce

Laura Jobin lays it on the line and captures the story behind the story of Leavenworth. The Los Angeles Times *once wrote about Laura that she "...abandoned the corporate world of high finance and high pressure, traded her sports car for a four-wheel drive truck and now reigns as top kick at the Leavenworth Chamber of Commerce. Miss the old life? 'You gotta be kidding,' she says."*

Here's Archie Marlin again with his peanut brittle. This time the proceeds made it possible to send our delegation to Milwaukee, Wisconsin to compete for—and win!—the All America City Award.

Now with Leavenworth's success, will corporate businesses come, and will this bring a depersonalization of the business core?

The new prosperity has created a solid financial base for the city government, which enables the town to accomplish a wider variety of projects and more ambitious ones, as well as to benefit from state and federal programs. However, it would be a great loss to the community if one result of its success was less direct involvement in problem solving by individual citizens. The inspiration for Bavarian Leavenworth was furthered largely because we were poor, lacked experience and professional know-how and were perhaps too proud to ask any government body for financial aid. People cared, and cared deeply enough to risk personal loss and failure, to make sacrifices, to overcome personality differences—literally to do it themselves. Out of selfless motives came great energy and creativity. So somehow everyone must continue to be willing to keep open the doors that sometimes seem to separate them—not just the doors between the city government, city council, building owners and merchants, but between the individual townspeople with all their diversity.

Nearly everything I've talked about in this book has happened through the spirit of giving among those who fixed their sights in a positive direction, knowing within themselves that the impossible could be done. People repeatedly found ways to rise above obstacles, disappointments, personality clashes and egotism for the good of one another and of the town.

As major problems appeared, someone usually took the lead to find a solution and then the other townspeople joined in. Where project studies were necessary, we undertook them ourselves—without experienced professionals. When money was needed for travel, printing and other expenses, we just dug into our pockets and came up with the cash without even writing these donations off our taxes!

Many of the non-profit groups were able to raise money by selling goods and services at various festivals, auctions and other fund-raising events. Shopkeepers who may have been selling these same items didn't look on such projects as competition, as they might well have done. They were willing to share the tourist dollar with such groups because they knew both the business community and the town benefited.

Often newcomers, as well as old timers, want to leave their mark on the town in some way, and many have wonderful ideas for improvements. However, some feel that now that they have arrived in Leavenworth, no further changes or population growth should occur. A few people here, as anywhere, seem to object to change of any kind. But change is inevitable and essential and, if handled properly, it can be exciting, as well as affording an opportunity for the healthy development of Leavenworth.

New Dreamers, New Projects

Through all the years that Bob and I lived in Leavenworth, our crowning dream was that there be a Bavarian castle near the river. We had a few designs drawn up for this castle, to be located at the south end of Eighth Street downtown. Now other "dreamers" are planning different castles for the Leavenworth area, one or two of which may become reality.

Before Bob and I decided to sell our waterfront property, we engaged Heinz Ulbricht to draw up the preliminary plans for many other projects—not just for the offstreet parking previously discussed, but also for a performing arts center, hotels, condominiums, a new city hall and a library at the south end of Ninth Street on our property. Upon our retirement, however, we sold this property to Vacation Internationale, a firm that builds and manages time share condominiums. That venture will attract substantial numbers of new people from many different parts of the country for a wonderful week or

Above. Environmental philantropist Harriet Bullitt. Her creative projects in Leavenworth will be a major influence on cultural developments in the whole Pacific Northwest. Below. The Boyd family's preliminary architectural drawings of a possible future resort in downtown Leavenworth.

two in Leavenworth. (Vacation Internationale Vice President Bob Ringgenberg is one of those who hopes to find someone with the imagination and resources to build a castle—at the end of Eighth Street.)

Today, there are several other projects that have been completed recently or are on the drawing board.

• Harriet Bullitt has transformed a former Catholic children's camp, located at the edge of town, into the Sleeping Lady Retreat and Conference Center. Sleeping Lady (taking its name from the mountain profile overlooking the site) is located on 70 acres of forest and meadow at the base of Icicle Canyon. The center is a first class, state-of-the-art facility that incorporates a multimillion dollar performing arts center with a concert hall that will attract world-class performers, and Leavenworth's first museum, with historical exhibits honoring Leavenworth's history, particularly the lives of Native Americans.

Harriet Bullitt has called herself an environmental philantropist, and her project is receiving national publicity as a trend setter because of her energy-saving approach to construction and ultimate operation. As *The Echo* reported: "From day one, Bullitt's order was to approach the reconstruction without wasting precious raw materials, sparing the destruction of old-growth stands...and installing systems that cared for the environment first."

Sleeping Lady's goal is to provide the best possible setting for creative thought and planning. In the summer, hikers can enjoy endless trails and the

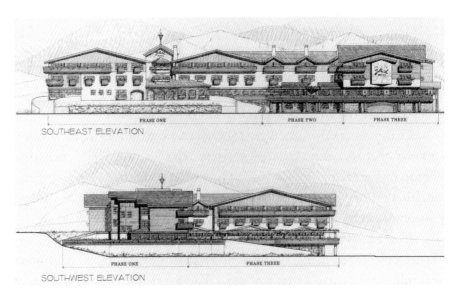

SOUTHEAST ELEVATION

SOUTHWEST ELEVATION

Icicle River and in winter, cross-country skiers can go from the cabin doorstep onto miles of groomed Nordic and skate tracks through the forest. As Harriet Bullitt says, "Sleeping Lady is a place to clear the cobwebs of the mind, to listen to the sounds of nature, and to the thoughts of companions, and to one's own creative voices."

• Bob Johnson and his son Rob, partners for twenty-one years, are planning to build an authentic Bavarian village on beautiful Mountain Home. Situated on 440 acres five miles from downtown Leavenworth, this hamlet will have some thirty buildings—mostly oriented toward recreation, for it will still rely on Leavenworth for all its services. The buildings will include a church, a first-class hotel, a restaurant, bed and breakfast houses and sundry shops for visitors. The Johnsons envisage building a dramatic castle, one that will be highly visible from downtown Leavenworth. If it is feasible, they want to build a small-gauge railroad with a steam engine, perhaps a cog-wheel train, again in European style.

Recreational facilities will include an 18-hole championship golf course, tennis courts and racquetball courts that will also be used for basketball, volleyball and other sports. A stream now runs through this scenic mountain valley, so they plan to create three lakes to capture the large mountain runoffs in the spring and reserve them for summer use, thus solving a major environmental issue. They will reforest the unused mountainside in pine and Douglas fir trees.

Although it will be several years before their dream is finally complete, Rob Johnson says, "It's not a project that we feel we have to do or we need to do. It's just something that's in our heart, that we want to do...to try and keep the theme alive...something we feel people would really enjoy."

• Another major project being proposed at this writing is one spearheaded by Richard Zucktriegel and an investor group. Their plan is to convert the downtown Leavenworth Fruit Company warehouses into a complex that would include a convention center, a heritage museum, a skating rink, parking facilities and theaters for plays and movies. All construction would be carried out in the Bavarian theme, with the warehouses possibly transformed into a Leavenworth castle.

• The Best Western Icicle Inn downtown has opened a new Family Fun Center called Icicle Junction. Over an extensive area adjoining the motel grounds, the owners have dredged a lagoon where people can enjoy

Bob (left) and son Rob Johnson play the Alp horn from the restaurant balcony of Rob's Enzian Motor Inn each morning at 8:15 and 9:15, while inside the guests enjoy a sumptuous breakfast. Bob's interest in the Alp horn has led him to craft horns himself and to play in an Alp horn quartet. Below. Nola Johnson has worked with husband Bob in designing the buildings and homes he and their son Rob have constructed. Nola is regarded as a savy businesswoman, whose kindness cheers fellow townspeople and visitors alike.

Owen and Pauline Watson are longtime residents who were leaders in the transformation of Leavenworth into a Bavarian village. The Alpen Rose Inn is their most recent project. Behind the inn is a remarkable flower garden, installed for the enjoyment of their guests.

bumperboats, and there will be an excursion train, an ice skating area, a Bavarian theme 18-hole miniature golf course and an activity center.

• Rob Johnson will open a championship 18-hole putting course on a stretch of land between his Enzian Motel and the Wenatchee River downtown. The design of this 72-par course will be in keeping with the aesthetics of the town; it will feature low-level lighting for nighttime playing and a waterfall and will be surrounded by mountain flowers.

My Own Dreams for Leavenworth's Future

Even though I no longer live in Leavenworth, my heart remains there and I often think about its future. As the old saying goes, "There's no harm in dreaming," so here are some of the things I dream about.

It's of aesthetic importance that Leavenworth's retail core area be expanded toward the Waterfront Park and the river. (Current zoning permits this to happen.) If such expansion occurred, a real walking town could be created— one that would show off the beauty of the surrounding landscape and take full advantage of the town's river and mountain views. In my opinion, new buildings should be oriented toward these views and the downtown streets should become walking streets like those found in many European towns.

Perhaps one day Leavenworth will have an underground or overhead pedestrian walkway to cross Highway 2. Perhaps a street or two will even be bridged a safe distance above traffic, and the bridges will be lined with shops and small cafes. Moreover, a beautiful bridge, modeled after the famous Ponte Vecchio (Old Bridge) in Florence, Italy, might span the river.

Another long-held dream of many is a tramway up one of the nearby mountains, and yet another of mine is that one day soon Leavenworth will have a beautiful Old European fountain downtown, possibly one that children and adults can play in during the summer months.

Meanwhile, service businesses such as grocery stores, hardware stores, drug stores and laundromats, which have given way to tourist-oriented businesses in the downtown core, need their own well-planned, special area with plenty of parking, so they can better serve local people without interfering with the visitors.

Parking—A Big Headache !

In my estimation, one of the biggest headaches for Leavenworth, especially for its visitors, is the lack of adequate parking. Over the years I've had different ideas about solving the parking dilemma and have tried various means to bring them about, but nothing seemed to work out and I'm afraid that my attempts to force the issue sometimes created hard feelings among important people in the community.

From the beginning I felt that the business community should lead the way in creating an organized parking project, preferably in one location. A "walking town" needs very selective offstreet parking in the downtown core area and possibly underground parking garages to retain the Old Bavarian atmosphere.

In 1965 Danish Solvang faced this problem and created S.M.I.D., the Solvang Municipal Improvement District, a project in which the business community purchased offstreet parking lots in the downtown area. As early as 1966 we had developed some ideas for a parking project but we needed legal consultation and were going to continue to need it. Here again, there was no money to pay for it, so we contacted J. Harold Anderson, a lawyer in Cashmere, Washington, and asked him how we could legally accomplish our offstreet parking goals with no support from the city.

Harold is the epitome of what every lawyer should be. He was so supportive of our aims that he donated his time and legal advice and drew up every legal document that was needed. Because the city council did not seem to be in tune with our goals, Harold advised that we set up a profit-making corporation but operate it as a non-profit organization. This would insure free parking for visitors.

At a meeting of downtown property owners and merchants, we took Harold's advice and voted to form ABC, the Alpine Betterment Corporation, and asked for $100-per-share investments. Vern Herrett became our first ABC president and took the lead by selling the group a piece of property for $3,750, consisting of two and one-half downtown lots, totaling 75 feet by 105 feet. Vern gave the group very easy terms, then helped us raise the money for the purchase!

Even before ABC bought the first parking lot, Bob and I turned over to the group an option to purchase a second property for offstreet parking. The property on which we took out an option for $7,000 was owned by Viva Sweat and consisted of at least four lots and one house. When the 100-day option was about to expire, we persuaded the ABC to sell more shares of stock to raise money to exercise it.

ABC was only a temporary and partial solution to providing offstreet parking, however. For years it operated in the red, because its funds were drained purchasing the property, graveling lots, providing maintenance and covering other expenses related to taxes, insurance, snow plowing and so on.

It is unbelievable how much merchant support ABC received, yet some business people refused to buy shares of stock or participate in any way. Some said they were not in the tourist business, others claimed the town really didn't need any more parking. Eventually it was impossible for ABC to continue acting as a non-profit group with the stockholders providing free offstreet parking for the town. To pay its debts, ABC sold the smaller of the two parking lots and divided the more than $100,000 profit among the stockholders—most of whom had purchased the stock originally only for the good of Leavenworth. The remaining lot owned by ABC later served as parking for downtown merchants, who rented the parking spaces by the month. ABC Shareholders now has become a profit-making corporation receiving high returns.

About 1990 I sent a letter to the Leavenworth City Council, with a copy to *The Echo*, offering to donate a large piece of land to serve as an underground parking facility. Located practically in the center of town, this property had been valued into the hundreds of thousands of dollars. The only

GROUP ADVERTISING

Beginning in the mid-1960s Leavenworth received a steady flow of free promotion and publicity for almost every major activity that was undertaken. However, by 1970 Bob and I felt the town needed a small group to create more effective publicity and to promote Leavenworth in various inexpensive ways. The group could operate as a group advertising subcommittee of the Leavenworth Chamber of Commerce Merchants Committee. About 1971 Bob Rodgers became chairman of the Merchants Committee and created the subcommittee.

This group sent out press releases far and wide and participated in television programs. Its members approached each business for financial support earmarked for advertising the town. The few thousand dollars raised was a modest budget to work with, so the committee targeted nearby areas like Puget Sound, where the best results could be obtained for a small investment.

Donations for publicity were strictly voluntary, however, and the same business people carried group advertising year after year, causing many supporters to resent those who would not give.

Something had to be done to lighten this financial burden, so group advertising was dropped, chamber membership dues were increased and a chamber manager was hired. Later, dues were increased still more and the highly qualified Laura Jobin became manager. Laura has done a truly great job and she seems to be the perfect choice as a representative for Leavenworth.

conditions for this gift were that Bob and I approve the plans for any structure built on it, that the design be harmonious with the Bavarian theme and that the project be developed in a reasonable time frame. Moreover, I offered to meet with the city and any others to discuss possible financing of the construction and ideas for maintaining the parking garage and providing environmental safeguards for the facility.

To my complete bewilderment I did not then or in the ensuing months receive a reply to my offer, or even an acknowledgement of the proposed gift.

LIFE IN LEAVENWORTH

For many years Leavenworth and the surrounding communities have been remarkably free of crime. In the early 1960s so few people were arrested that the city jail was closed and the police staff let go. The town engaged the services of the county sheriff and turned the former jail into a storage area for the city.

Today, one of the most read columns in *The Leavenworth Echo* is the "Sheriff's Report" which lists every call received during the week. Although there are the occasional reports of theft and burglary, drunken and disorderly conduct and other relatively minor criminal behavior, the local citizens enjoy a peaceful atmosphere. These items are taken from recent entries in the "Sheriff's Report"—

A woman reported a suspicious subject prowling the area. An investigating deputy discovered he was a 65-year old retired dentist interested in purchasing real estate in the area.

An Eagle Creek man reported loud classical music.

Speeding forklifts were reported in Dryden.

A disoriented woman was discovered taking a nap in a goats' pen in Tumwater Canyon.

Two neighbors reported a loud party on the Chumstick Highway. The couple celebrating its 60th wedding anniversary advised deputies they would settle down at 10 P.M.

Several months passed until, hearing nothing from the city, I withdrew the offer and sold the land to Vacation Internationale, which had made a proposal to buy it.

Since the late 1960s various committees have studied the parking problem, and each one has come up with recommendations. But then nothing happened. Eventually another study was requested, and its conclusions also went unheeded. The city has paid for a study of the parking problem once again, the results of which were published in 1995. Primarily, the recommendations were that merchants and their staff walk or bike to work.

Over the years merchants and their employees have been asked to park off Front Street at least a block away from downtown buildings. If a parking facility is located any distance from town, a conveyance could be provided to shuttle the visitors back and forth. Perhaps a solution might be to use about three acres in or near Enchantment Park, just upstream from Blackbird Island, landscape it properly and find a way to provide security without undue expense. What a wonderful way to enter town—a short stroll over Blackbird Island, over a corner of Waterfront Park. And of course a shuttle service could be provided from that area as well.

To my mind a real threat in solving the parking problem would come with the creation of mini-mall-type parking areas. This would destroy the Old Bavarian village atmosphere and make a walking town an impossibility. Is Leavenworth up to the challenge of providing the needed offstreet parking without wrecking the environment—or the pocketbook? It has certainly been a perennial headache, but the people will find a solution. Perhaps another dreamer will point the way!

Maintaining High Standards—The Key to Future Success

Whatever projects people dream up in the future—it is vital that they incorporate high-quality Bavarian design. Consequently, the efforts of the Leavenworth Design Review Board must be supported.

High-quality Bavarian design is just as necessary for city government buildings as for private ventures. And it must be applied to everything the eye can see. Old lamp standards and all signs must continue to be in keeping with the Old Bavarian theme. Buildings outlined in lights can't have burned-out bulbs—a problem that can be solved largely by using long-lasting bulbs. In the fall, autumn leaves should be fresh looking, so they must be cut and brought in each weekend. And—surely one of the biggest secrets to everyone's enjoyment of Leavenworth—bountiful displays of flowers must be incorporated into all designs for new facilities!

Aside from design matters, another secret of future success lies in customer service. Business people must continue to give very good values on high-quality merchandise, be friendly and helpful to customers and keep their stores clean and inviting. Also, it is important to find new merchandise, rather

"[Leavenworth has] now become a destination point, instead of just a drop-in like it was. When we first started, of course, people would drive by and see it was different and stop. And now there are people traveling many miles just to come to Leavenworth!"
— Owen Watson

173

Both pages. With Leavenworth's phenomenal growth, it is essential to continue to strive for authenticity to maintain an Old Bavarian atmosphere. The Planning Commission and the Design Review Board both deserve special recognition and our gratitude for ensuring that all new and remodeled business buildings follow established guidelines, including strict sign control measures. Even fast food chains and service stations adhere to these standards, in both architecture and signage.

"The idea that people can do these things for them-selves. That was the beauty of it....as things grow and change, they must be [approached] in a way that reflects the integrity of what we have....and we need to continue to maintain our tradition and high quality....I think it is critical that we keep alive the story of Leavenworth and how it began.... quality is essential in order to maintain what we have here."
— *Jane Turnbull*

than copy what is sold next door or down the street. There should be more specialty shops with unique merchandising ideas that fit the Old Bavarian atmosphere.

The visitor dollars spent in Leavenworth have skyrocketed, and new motels and other businesses have opened and prospered. Others have closed, claiming disasters such as the great fire of 1994, temporary road closures and so on. Many businesses starting in Leavenworth have invited failure due to under financing, poor selection of merchandise, unappealing or dirty stores or the attitude that all the owners have to do is open their doors and they will become wealthy. The challenge to merchants and service ventures is to provide something unique, not just to copy what others have found successful.

So long as the people of Leavenworth strive for authenticity, citizen involvement, community pride and genuine friendliness to visitors, they will insure Leavenworth's future success.

Helping Other Towns

Representatives from towns throughout the nation and abroad continue to come seeking advice and suggestions for developing a theme town. Those of us who have been approached have freely shared our experiences to help them find their own way. When we are invited to speak to other towns, we always urge others not to copy what we did but to study their own community closely and look to themselves for creative inspiration and direction. I would urge the people of Leavenworth to actively reach out to other towns and offer whatever help they can, remembering that they are helping others to help themselves.

Some towns like Kellogg, Idaho and White Salmon, Washington seem to have actually copied the Leavenworth theme, but this imitation should not be considered a threat. From our earliest days at The Squirrel Tree, and later with our shops in Leavenworth, we never feared competition—we only needed to be concerned with doing our very best.

Leavenworth at a Crossroads

As Leavenworth enters the late 1990s, many of the townspeople I've interviewed have expressed a concern that "Leavenworth is at a crossroads." This may well be so. Residential and business real estate prices continue to accelerate at unbelievable rates. Housing has become so expensive that the people needed to support the businesses and industries cannot afford to live in Leavenworth.

Perhaps in the forefront in meeting this growing dilemma is Rev. Carl Florea, who for ten years has worked to keep Leavenworth "both a healthy, growing economy and also a healthy, growing community." Along with finding ways to provide affordable housing, there is the question of housing developments spreading over the valley and hillsides. I hope to see instead clustered residential developments in Old Bavarian designs, which would also give preference to open spaces. Besides providing enjoyment for people, this solution would afford a natural habitat for wildlife. "The biggest problem," says Rev. Florea, "is whether we address having housing (for) the people who choose to live here and work here.... What I think is the crossroads—and the battle—is for the soul of Leavenworth as a community."

"I think the greatest challenge is still ahead of us—that somehow we have got to figure out how to have growth, and yet how to keep being a village. The magic of Leavenworth, to me, has been that it is a place where we live! And if people come, they know it as a place where people really, genuinely live! It's not just a tourist attraction that closes at five o'clock or whatever.

... and [yet we must] still be able to accommodate growth and all of the people and guests that we anticipate will come. And hope will come! That's going to take some real imagination, and some real thought!"

— Pauline Watson

Leavenworth valley is nearly four miles long and one mile wide. Mountain elevations around Leavenworth vary—some are over a mile high. Mt. Rainier is in the background (center).

"Leavenworth offers a lot of outdoor activitity—climbing and hiking and camping...good fishing and hunting. They have cross-country ski courses. Everything is offered! It's a beautiful area to live in!"

— Mike Brickert

A Miracle
of Giving

*"Truly Leavenworth is a gift from God—a miracle that began with
the creation of the area's natural surroundings, grew with a vision of
what to do with them and multiplied every time individuals gave of
themselves to help that vision become a reality. This miracle of giving is
the theme and underlying reason for our success.*

*Why do people like Leavenworth so much? It's because Leavenworth
GIVES so much!"*

*—From my presentation to the 1979
annual Leavenworth Chamber of Commerce dinner*

In 1979 Ken Marson, president of the Leavenworth Chamber of Commerce, asked me to prepare a special program for the annual chamber
dinner. He thought we should have a visual presentation that would help
townspeople feel proud of all their accomplishments in creating this Bavarian village. So Bob Rodgers and I, with the assistance of Tim Easterly
and Harry Butcher, produced a slide presentation on the transformation
of Leavenworth. Tim suggested we title it "Leavenworth—A Miracle of
Giving." He clearly saw that the real story of Bavarian Leavenworth was
about people who gave and gave and gave. It was about spiritual love. In a
recent interview with Tim, he recalled:

*"A Miracle of Giving" seemed to capture a lot of the essence of what
Ted's idea [was]...the power, I guess, behind a lot of this. It's that you
can give the architecture, the festivals, the bandstand and all the things
that were created...free of charge.*

*The miracle of that of course is twofold: One is that people respond by
coming and enjoying it and being a part of it, so that it makes it a success.*

The other part of it is probably not so obvious, but it's what happens inside of each person as they learn that it is the miracle of giving that really makes it happen. The summation of it is, as we are told in the Bible, "But he that is greatest among you shall be your servant." (Matthew 23:11)

I think it's the central core issue that threads itself through the whole story of Leavenworth. And that is, that you really give of yourself in whatever way you can, and then in all kinds of different ways that's returned back to you. It's in the doing of it itself!

Getting there isn't half the fun—it's all the fun! The essence of it all is the process. That's why you can't compromise principle for any kind of expedient.

And I think the essence of Bob and Ted's life—and Ted particularly in the way he has gone about that whole process through these years—exemplifies a lot of that....

Leavenworth's transformation has been a gift to every visitor to the town. It has also provided countless opportunities for the townspeople themselves—opportunities for creativity, for selfless giving, for working together in overcoming seemingly insurmountable obstacles and for practicing forgiveness.

Leavenworth is blessed with so many natural assets—the mountains, the forests and rivers, the beauties of the four seasons. Most residents have done all that they could to preserve these resources by not polluting the air, waters and soil. In the beginning we were given the mountains and forests and wildlife. In Leavenworth we found a way to improve our natural assets—economically feasible ways at that!

One of our greatest pleasures as we watched our dreams come true was the discovery of just how fantastic people really are when they work together for the common good.

Whenever I met with representatives of other communities, they invariably asked, "What was your single biggest problem?" They assumed it was a lack of money, or professional know-how or something else. But my answer always was *the human ego*.

It is my personal feeling that one of the biggest obstacles in the pathway of progress and maturity is self. It was nothing more than our egos that brought on most of our difficulties. It was our egos that at times led us into greed, resentment of one another, envy, jealousy, destructive gossip and ruthless competition rather than cooperation. It has been the same ego that at times has misrepresented the story of Leavenworth and is most responsible for stopping or nearly stopping every worthwhile project.

Yet in spite of anything and everything, so many people gave knowledge, skills, money, time, effort and material goods to make these dreams become realities. Within them was what I call "a living spirit" which is in every person and which can work miracles. This spirit enabled us to survive all obstacles, and it is just as alive today as it has ever been. As many people have said, "Someone or something certainly has been looking after us to bring everything together at the right time."

Whoever and whatever was needed for the good of Leavenworth usually appeared at the right moment as if by magic—someone with new ideas, with needed finances, with professional or technical skills or with hard-working helping hands for community projects. The right leaders were always present. If a political leader wasn't right, he or she could be removed, even if it took a write-in vote. If we needed property, it would appear. If it was money, it would pour in—hundreds of thousands of dollars. If it was publicity, it arrived on schedule. And all of this came to Leavenworth free, without any strings.

Over the years this little village that was nearly a ghost town has enriched the hearts and minds of millions of visitors, while amply providing for those who worked to make it all happen. Although it will never be possible to name everyone who contributed to the transformation, I'd like to give a few examples.

When Russ Lee and his family agreed to publish the special free edition of *The Leavenworth Echo* to serve as a publicity brochure for the town, they did it without a profit motive, for the good of the town they loved. Townspeople volunteered to write stories about the area. More volunteers helped sell advertising so that the paper could be printed and distributed free of charge. As the thousands of newspapers rolled off the press, they had to be hand folded, so more volunteers appeared. Finally, willing volunteers carried the paper out of town on business and pleasure trips to distribution points where they could be picked up by travelers. From the beginning Russ and Vera Lee freely devoted generous newspaper coverage to the festivals and events in Leavenworth, and later publishers of *The*

"We can see the vision of it and ...although we're beginning to get to the age where we ought to think of retiring, there's no way I can think of retiring. I keep seeing so many things to do. I can see how great it is. I just see God's hand in everything that has happened."
—Nola Johnson

Russ Lee, the publisher and editor of The Leavenworth Echo *for 18 years who, with his wife Vera, never wavered in championing the vision of a Bavarian Leavenworth. Today Russ continues to serve the community through volunteer work at the senior citizen center.*

Echo—Earl Petersen and Ron Hindman, Lee and Peggy Lathrop, Miles and Jane Turnbull, Ren and Adrienne Adam, Jim and Amy Davis and Jeff and Liz Gauger—have continued this true community support.

We might also recall Project LIFE, Project Alpine, the festivals, Art in the Park, the flowers, the beautification and clean-up efforts, restoration and replacement of the downtown lampposts, the parks, the bandstand and so many other improvements. Whenever there was a need that seemed impossible to meet, money and know-how often appeared seemingly out of thin air.

The epitome of the indefinable spirit that made Leavenworth succeed can be found in the life of Carolyn Schutte. As former mayor Wilbur Bon said, all the things she "helped us do would never have gotten done if not for her." Carolyn's was the true charity of spiritual love, for she demonstrated that the greatest way to give is to give in secret. The essence of a miracle has to do with giving as well as receiving. Through her deep spiritual awareness, Carolyn knew that every one of us is the perfect child of God. Her life itself was a gift of love and forgiveness.

The inspiration for giving and sharing comes from a higher source and it manifests itself in an infinite number of ways through ordinary people like you and Bob and me and the people of Leavenworth, Washington—indeed, through people everywhere!

Left. The Oregon Historical Society complex in Portland, Oregon, with its trompe l'oeil by the world famous artist Richard Haas. Below. In 1988 three executives from the Society are guests at the historic Haus Lorelei in Leavenworth. (From left) Leavenworth Mayor Will Martinell, OHS representatives Louis Flannery, Rick Harmon and Jim Strassmaier and me.

THE PRICE & RODGERS HISTORICAL LEAVENWORTH COLLECTION

In the near future the Theodore H. Price and Robert F. Rodgers Historical Leavenworth Collection will be donated to The Oregon Historical Society, located in Portland, Oregon. The collection includes hundreds of photographs, slides, videotapes, films, and audiotapes; newspapers; architectural plans; maps; copies of reports; correspondence; property records and invoices; research notes and miscellaneous artifacts.

Among the features of the collection are first-person accounts, in video and audio recordings, of many who participated in the revitalization of Leavenworth, as well as present-day interviews with those actively engaged in furthering Leavenworth's development. Included are interviews with Bob Rodgers and an oral history of Ted Price.

The Oregon Historical Society has one of the region's finest research libraries. Its archives and exhibits deal primarily with the Pacific Northwest, but also cover the entire Pacific Rim. The OHS facilities include a museum, exhibit galleries, the research library, an advanced oral history department, a photographic library and a bookstore.

Index

Photo Credits

Unless otherwise noted, photo credits are from left to right and top to bottom on each page. Photographs courtesy of the Thomas L. Greene, Jr. Historical Collection are indicated by "Greene Collection." Photographs from the Price & Rodgers Historical Leavenworth Collection are indicated by "P & R."

PRELIMINARY PAGES. Title page, photo by Richard Barrington. Page viii, photo by Cliff Ellis, courtesy of the Smith-Western Postcard Company. Page ix, photo by Michael W. Siegrist, Sr. Pages x-xii, photos by Richard Barrington. Page xiii, photos by Richard Barrington; (top right) and (left center) photos by Michael W. Siegrist, Sr. Page xiv, photos by Richard Barrington; (bottom) photo by Michael W.Siegrist, Sr. Page xv, Photos by Richard Barrington; (bottom) photo by Dr. Bob Smith, courtesy of the Leavenworth Chamber of Commerce. Page xvi and xx, photos by Walt Rembold.

CHAPTER 1. Page 2, photo by Walt Rembold; (bottom) photo by Richard Barrington.

CHAPTER 2. Page 4, photo by Steve Nickols. Pages 6-9, Courtesy of Greene Collection. Pages 11-16, P & R.

CHAPTER 3. Page 18, P & R. Page 19, (Left and top right) photos by Walt Rembold; (below right) photo, P & R. Page 20, photo by Walt Rembold. Page 21, Top left, photo courtesy of *The Wenatchee Daily World*; other photos by Walt Rembold. Page 22, photo by Walt Rembold. Pages 23-27, P & R. Page 28, courtesy of *The Wenatchee Daily World*. Pages 30-31, P & R.

CHAPTER 4. Pages 34-35, P & R. Page 36, courtesy of *The Leavenworth Echo*; photo by Walt Rembold. Page 39, photo by Walt Rembold, courtesy of *The Seattle Times*. Page 41, Photo by Bob Miller, courtesy of Chuck Bergman Collection and Leavenworth Chamber of Commerce. Page 42, P & R. Page 45, Photo by Walt Rembold. Page 46, P & R. Page 48, P & R; (lower) photo by Walt Rembold. Page 49, P & R. Page 51, Photo by Walt Rembold.

CHAPTER 5. Page 54, Courtesy of *The Leavenworth Echo*. Page 57, Sketch by designer Earl Petersen. Page 59, photos by Walt Rembold. Page 60, photo by Richard Barrington. Page 61, Sketch by designer Heinz Ulbricht.

CHAPTER 6. Page 62, Courtesy of *The Leavenworth Echo*. Page 64, design by Earl Petersen; (lower) design by Heinz Ulbricht; (bottom) photo by Walt Rembold. Pages 65-66 and 68, photos by Walt Rembold. Page 69-70, photos by Richard Barrington. Page 71, Top left and center, photos by Walt Rembold; sketch by Robert F. Rodgers; (bottom) photo by Richard Barrington. Page 72, photo by Michael W. Siegrist, Sr. Pages 73-76 and 78, photos by Walt Rembold. Page 79, P & R.

CHAPTER 7. Page 80, Courtesy of *The Seattle Times*. Page 82, Photo by Richard Barrington. Pages 84-85, photos by Walt Rembold. Page 86, P & R. Page 88, Photos by Walt Rembold; (far lower left) photo by Richard Barrington. Page 89, Photos by Richard Barrington. Pages 90-91, Before remodeling photos by Walt Rembold; after remodeling photos by Richard Barrington. Pages 92-93, Center spread photo by Richard Barrington. Page 92, Bottom photos, P & R. Page 93, Top right, 3 photos before remodeling, Greene Collection; (lower right) photo by Walt Rembold; (left bottom) P & R; (center bottom) photo by Richard Barrington. Pages 94, photos by Richard Barrington, except (center, far left and far right) photos by Jeanne E. Galick. Page 95, photos by Richard Barrington. Page 96, Top, Greene Collection; (center) photo by Walt Rembold; (bottom) photo by Richard Barrington. Page 97, Top left and center, photos by Walt Rembold; (right) photo by Richard Barrington; (lower right) photo by Jeanne E. Galick. Page 98, P & R. Page 99, (Top) courtesy of *The Leavenworth Echo*; courtesy of *The Wenatchee Daily World*. Pages 100 and 102, P & R.

CHAPTER 8. Page 104, photo by Richard Barrington. Page 106, P & R. Page 107, photo by Jeanne E. Galick. Page 108, photo by Walt Rembold. Page 109, (Center) courtesy of *The Leavenworth Echo*; (right) P & R. Page 110, photo by Walt Rembold. Page 111, photos by Jim Corwin. Page 113, photo by Richard Barrington. Page 114, Top, P & R; (center right) photo by Jim Corwin; (lower left and right) photos by Richard Barrington. Page 115, Top left, photo by Don Eastman; (right,top to bottom) 4 photos by Richard Barrington; (bottom left) photo by Jim Corwin. Page 116, Top left, P & R.; photos by Richard Barrington. Page 117, Top left, photo by Richard Barrington; (top right and bottom) photos by Michael W. Siegrist, Sr. Page 118, Top left and right, P & R; (bottom) photo by Richard Barrington. Page 119, photos by Richard Barrington; except (far right center) P & R. Page 120, (Top left) P & R; (top right) photo by Walt Rembold; (center and bottom) photos by Richard Barrington. Page 121, photo by Richard Barrington. Page 122, P & R. Page 124, Top photo by Richard Barrington; (lower) P & R. Page 125, P & R. Page 126, photos by Richard Barrington. Page 127, photo by Eleanor Culling. Page 128, P & R.

CHAPTER 9. Page 130, photo by Walt Rembold. Page 132, Top photo by Walt Rembold; (bottom) photo by Steve Nickols. Page 134, Design by Talley & Associates. Pages 135-136, P & R. Page 137, photos by Richard Barrington. Page 138, Photos by Walt Rembold; except (top right) P & R. Page 139, Top left and right, photos by Richard Barrington; (right center) photo courtesy of the Leavenworth Chamber of Commerce; (bottom) photo by Walt Rembold. Page 140, photo by Richard Barrington. Pages 141-142, P & R. Page 143, photo by Richard Barrington. Page 144, Rod Simpson design for 1971 Comprehensive Recreation Plan. Page 145, P & R. Page 146, P & R. Page 147, photo by Walt Rembold. Pages 148-149, P & R. Pages 150-152, photos by Richard Barrington.

CHAPTER 10. Page 154, courtesy of *The Leavenworth Echo*. Page 155, photo by Richard Barrington. Page 156, Courtesy of *The Leavenworth Echo*. Page 157, photo by Francisco J. Rangel. Page 159, photo by Walt Rembold. Pages 160-161 (Top center) courtesy of *The Leavenworth Echo*; remaining photos, P & R. Page 162, Top left, courtesy of the Leavenworth Chamber of Commerce; (top center) courtesy of Eleanor Culling; (top right) photo by Richard Barrington; (center far right) photo by Michael W. Siegrist, Sr.; remaining photos, P & R. Page 163, courtesy of Laura Jobin. Page 164, photo by Walt Rembold. Page 165, courtesy of artist June Schoenhofen; (right) courtesy of designer Heinz Ulbricht. Page 166, P & R; designs courtesy of Lyman Boyd. Page 167, Top photo by Richard Barrington; (lower) P & R. Page 168, Courtesy of Owen and Pauline Watson; (right) photo by Richard Barrington. Pages 174-176, photos by Richard Barrington.

CHAPTER 11. Page 178, photo by Walt Rembold. Page 182, Courtesy of Russell Lee. Page 183, Courtesy of the Oregon Historical Society; (lower) courtesy of *The Leavenworth Echo*.

ORDER ADDITIONAL COPIES OF

MIRACLE TOWN

A Perfect Gift For Every Occasion

~

ORDER BEFORE JANUARY 2, 1997 FOR SPECIAL PRE-PUBLICATION PRICE
$19.95 Paperbound Edition
$35 Hardcover—*Limited Edition*—Numbered and Signed by the author
After January 2, 1997, $24.95 Paperbound, $40.00 Hardcover

QUANTITY ORDERS (12 or more copies) from non-profit organizations and other groups—community, business, religous and other. Write, giving details, for prices on bulk orders.

Send Orders, Checks and Inquiries to:
Price & Rodgers
P.O. Box 55, Leavenworth, Washington 98826

ORDER FORM

Quantity   Amount

_____ Paperback @ $19.95 ($24.95 after January 2, 1997). . . . . _____

_____ Hardcover @ $35.00 Numbered and Signed Edition ($40.00 after 1/2/97) . . . . _____

_____ Postage and Handling: $4.00 (Additional copies @ $2.00 each) . . . . _____

_____ Washington Residents Only: Add Sales Tax @ 8% . . . . _____

Payment by check, money order or credit card only   Order Total _____
CANADIAN/FOREIGN: Postal money orders in U. S. Currency

Visa or MasterCard Number _____

Expiration date:_____ Signature _____

Name _____ Phone _____

Address _____

City/State/Zip _____

Ship to: *(if different from above)* Name _____

Address _____

City/State/Zip _____